DO MONKEYS GO TO HEAVEN? 2.0

More Reflections on Finding God in All Creation

JOHN McCARTHY, SJ

NOVALIS

© 2017 Novalis Publishing Inc.

Cover design: Martin Gould
Cover images: Getty images
Layout: Audrey Wells
Interior images: Courtesy of John McCarthy, S.J., except pages 19, 78 and 120 (Jupiter Images), 48 (Mary McCarthy) and 111 (William Mbugua, S.J.)

Published by Novalis

Publishing Office
10 Lower Spadina Avenue, Suite 400
Toronto, Ontario, Canada
M5V 2Z2

Head Office
4475 Frontenac Street
Montréal, Québec, Canada
H2H 2S2

www.novalis.ca

Library and Archives Canada Cataloguing in Publication

McCarthy, John William, 1958-, author
    Do monkeys go to heaven 2.0 : more reflections on finding
God in all creation / Fr. John McCarthy, SJ.

ISBN 978-2-89688-410-0 (softcover)

    1. Creation. 2. Nature--Religious aspects--Christianity.
3. Spiritual life. 4. McCarthy, John William, 1958-. I. Title.

BT695.M332 2017   231.7'65   C2017-900412-3

Printed in Canada.

We acknowledge the support of the Government of Canada.

5   4   3   2   1   21   20   19   18   17

MIX
Paper from
responsible sources
FSC
www.fsc.org   FSC® C103567

TABLE OF CONTENTS

INTRODUCTION

"To make publicly known, to reveal, to divulge, to announce …." Thus, may one understand the Middle English roots of the verb "to publish." Three years ago, in 2014, the publisher took a chance on making known *Do Monkeys Go to Heaven?* – a collection of musings on science, nature and spirituality. Never did I imagine that a second volume would appear.

The invitation by Novalis Publishing to prepare a second volume of my reflections was a function of your response to the first volume. A generous response, I may add. Any author takes a risk in publishing. To reveal or divulge one's inner heart and mind, especially on paper, is always risky.

The foremost risk is obviously one of not being read. The book is announced to deaf ears. Short is its shelf life. Long is its oblivion. Happily, that was not to be the case for me. You awakened to the announcing and bought and – I dare hope – read the book.

A related risk is one of being misunderstood. An author reveals or divulges what's on his or her mind. Such thoughts are often nuanced, complex concepts that dance and weave rather than march and stride ahead. Words on a page are contained, in black and white. Why the words were written and how they are received may be miles apart. A published work has a life of its own. The writer has relinquished all control. Only the reader will decide the fate of the opus.

In effect, it was you, the reader, who decided that this second volume would see the light of day. It was not the publisher. For that, I bow in gratitude. I thank you.

I have been heartened by your feedback. For many, an initial desire to seek the answer to the question "Do monkeys go to heaven?" was replaced by a contemplative read of the various invitations. Many of you commented that the book invited a second, more reflective read. The book's initial accessibility opened one up to a depth of consideration. In reading the book a second time, you found more to like, more to think about, more to appreciate.

I am so happy to hear that many of you read the work again to reflect more deeply, to savour more sweetly. That's how I envisioned the various musings. They were meant to be exactly that – musings to invite the reader to depth, to attentiveness to the beauty and grandeur of our lives and our world, despite all evidence to the contrary. They were never meant to be prescriptions or well-defined codes of living. I suppose one could say the book was meant to be prayed, rather than read.

I hope you will relish this second collection of musings in the same manner. In reading my stories and encounters, you will also be reminded of yours. My journey is unique. It has its glory and its limitations. It does not define the world, but hopefully traces something of the beauty and glory of our lives – and of all creation.

And so, I offer you this second collection. Let me know what you think. If, in opening this book, you meet and mingle with something of your own story, well and good. We all have a richness of story that outshines the master writer. Be attentive to the river of life that flows, ever so deeply and silently, beneath the seeming banality and vulgarity of life. Still waters do indeed run deep. May these pages awaken you, even in some small way, to the grandeur of life.

John McCarthy, S.J.
April 1, 2017

ACKNOWLEDGEMENTS

A book is never a solo creation. This one is no exception. Joe Sinasac, publisher of Novalis, generously invited me to consider a second volume of reflections. Simon Appolloni, editorial director of Novalis, attentively crafted and shepherded the manuscript. As editor, Anne Louise Mahoney beautifully transformed the text. Matthew Sottile, marketing coordinator at Novalis, skillfully produced a promotional YouTube video for the book. I am grateful to Erica Zlomislić for generously proofreading the text.

The Very Reverend Peter Bisson, S.J., Provincial Superior of the Jesuits in English Canada, has supported my writing over the years. I am grateful to family and friends who unhesitatingly promoted the first volume of reflections.

Finally, to you, dear reader, for taking this book in hand. For what's a writer without a reader?

JANUARY

Catch, Cradle and Cherish

S t. Ignatius of Loyola (1491–1556), the founder of the Society of Jesus (Jesuits), was a master of human psychology long before we even knew the term.

A favourite spiritual exercise promoted by Ignatius has come to be known as the Examen. It is a simple but powerful daily prayer exercise and goes something like this.

At the end of the day, give yourself about 15 minutes to look over your day with the eyes of faith. Begin with a short prayer of thanksgiving for your life and for the day that has passed. Ask the Holy Spirit to enlighten you with the mystery and grace of the day.

Ask Jesus Christ to take you by the hand and to show you your day in his light. What we see and what God sees may be two different things. What we hear and what God hears are often not the same.

You may let Jesus Christ walk with you from the beginning of the day to your present moment in a chronological meander. Or you may find Christ inviting you to specific moments or feelings or thoughts from the day.

As you walk with Christ, he may call you to rest with a moment from your day. You may find yourself lingering, as if you were hand in hand with a lover on a soft, sultry summer evening. Or you may find yourself troubled, saddened, anxious, jolted by something from the day. These are special moments.

This is where Christ wishes to meet you. Catch those moments and hold them.

Rest with Christ as you would in the arms of a lover. Feel his presence, his warmth, his strength. Relish the moments of the day – the smell of freshly brewed coffee, the sprinkle of rain on your garden flowers, an experience of forgiveness, wonder, awe. Savour these moments, taste them, breathe them as the grace of God. Christ is calling you at that very moment to have eyes that see and ears that hear.

Christ may also invite you into the Garden of Gethsemane. Remember that gardens are also the havens of lovers, tucked away for lovers' delight. But this garden has in it pain and fear and sorrow. But God's will be done. Here Christ may wish to gift you with grace that comes from tears and sorrow. You may remember those times of the day when you refused the gift of the other, when you turned in on your fearful self and shut out the world. But remember, Christ is revealing these moments not to punish or repudiate, but to invite you to child-like abandon into his arms. These moments reveal our insatiable need for God and for others. We turn to God in sorrow and abandon, take Christ's hand and move forward.

A friend of mine once described the Examen as a way to "catch, cradle and cherish" the day that has gone before us. To cradle and to cherish our day with Jesus Christ at our side. What marvellous grace. Marvellous because we are no longer left to our own feeble pride or fear. We have a lover at our side, holding us closely, whispering to us the marvels of our day.

It has been said that life is just one damn thing after another. Don't let your days be like that. Call on Christ at the end of your day. Let him show you who you are. Let the Lover show you as the beloved.

A Record Snowfall – and Peace

One day several years ago, almost 40 centimetres of snow fell on my hometown of St. John's, Newfoundland. Apparently, it was a record snowfall, surpassing the 29.2 cm that fell on the city in 1946.

Growing up in St. John's, I would love it when a hefty snowstorm would shut down the city. For days, it seemed, the strong northeasterlies would blow in off the tempestuous North Atlantic. The seemingly relentless snow-laden howls whistled the wires, whitened the landscape and scurried through every drafty nook and cranny in our house.

If we were lucky, we would lose power. Somewhere down the line, in the back hinterland, some section of the towering hydro lines would succumb to the burden of snow, rime ice and wind. Down it would bend, honouring the power of the winds.

The impending darkness and cold would bring out our candles and huddle our family together in the living room. I delighted in those times. The laughter, the sense of coziness as the candles flickered in the impending coolness. We were warmed by this time together.

After the storm had passed, with abandonment and excitement we exited our shelters to find a city hushed to stillness. Maybe extirpation would be a better term, as we sometimes battled with the piles of snow heaving against our doors.

The normal outline of the city had been obliterated by the snow and wind. Where once roads provided passage, snow dunes now offered new routes for energetic young boys and girls. Tops of telephone poles had grown closer. Cars had disappeared.

What wonders had been created by the winds that piled snow in shape and form never imagined! The wind-hardened curves and crests created a dream world to our young eyes. New lands to explore, snow caves and tunnels to create, mountains to ascend and claim.

And the silence. Oh, what blessed, fulsome silence had fallen on the city of enterprise. Hushed: no planes in the sky, all cars frozen silent, with only a huddled human here and there, shovel in hand, beginning the long hours of release from the snowy tombs.

Many years later, while living in Vancouver, British Columbia, I was fine with the seemingly constant winter rain because I had the mountains covered in snow. The best of both worlds, one would say. At least you didn't have to shovel it, many a Vancouverite would profess. At the same time, I used to hanker for a hell of a good snow – the kind that shuts down a city and huddles people together.

Toblerone Spurned

I begrudgingly tossed several pieces of my beloved Toblerone onto the fresh snow. Out of the cold spruces and firs, they dropped to the ground, intent on their afternoon snack. To my surprise, my offer was snubbed, plain and simple. They would have nothing to do with Switzerland's finest.

The first one to reach the ground poked and picked at the cold chocolate. The other two never even tried – aware, it seems, of their sibling's rejection of my offer.

Ever since Toblerone first appeared in Bern, Switzerland, in 1868, I am sure this was the first and firmest snub of the chocolate delight. Not to be put off, I made a second attempt with some homemade banana bread. Within seconds, all my offerings had been consumed.

In Newfoundland, we call them whiskey jacks, or true to their name, camp robbers. Most people know them as gray jays or

Canada jays. "Whiskey jack" is probably an Anglicization of the Cree term *wisakedjak*, a demi-god that features significantly in Cree creation myths. As the trickster, the whiskey jack becomes a source of inspiration on how to live good lives. The gray jay has also become a symbol of good company. I can relate to that. In my many years of traipsing around in the boreal woods, the whiskey jack has been a constant and welcome companion. You never know when they'll appear. During a recent snowshoe jaunt in Newfoundland's boreal forest (where I lost some good Toblerone), they came all of a sudden, unannounced. The swish of wings brushing the stillness, the lovely quiet chirp. I'm often in the woods by myself, so the company is welcome. They follow along, panhandling, waiting for a handout.

It's special when they land on your hand to partake of your offerings. The grip of the claws, the dangling weight of the jay, the jab of the strong, black beak. Such things open us up to new worlds beyond our everyday experience. We need such things. They delight us, teach us and invite us to enter another creature's world. In such meetings, our world expands and we can never return to the former world of our own making. The world of the jay (and all else of nature) is beyond our fabrication and fixing. Any form of relation with the non-human world enriches and expands our horizons. It makes us more human.

A 2016 poll by the National Bird Project of the Royal Canadian Geographic Society nominated the gray jay as the national bird of Canada. With over 450 bird species to choose from, the whiskey jack must have had a lot going for it. It lives across Canada from coast to coast and stays here all winter. That is evidence of a true Canadian bird. No snowbird here! It lives in the cold boreal coniferous forests away from human settlement, and yet is well known for its friendliness and curiosity to all forest travellers and workers.

I left my offered Toblerone on the snowbank and continued on my way. The three of them followed me for the next hour or so. Hoping for some more of that sweet banana bread? Simply friendly and curious? Or maybe even intent that I find my way out of the woods under the waning daylight? Whatever the reason, it was good to have their company along the way.

As for the Toblerone, the Swiss chocolatier Jean Tobler (1830–1905) obviously didn't have the whiskey jack in mind when he invented his soon-to-be-famous chocolate treat. There's no doubt that the whiskey jack has a mind of its own. I look forward to our next rendezvous in some wood far, far away.

The Sound of Silence

"Listen," he said. "Just listen. Isn't it beautiful?"

A brother Jesuit and I were about an hour or so into our winter hike in Algonquin Provincial Park in Ontario. The sun sparkled. The snow lay white. The lake stood frozen.

I stopped, lowered my head – and listened.

What is it to listen to nothing? Can one hear no sound at all? That is just what we did in that moment. No breeze to stir the trees. No water to wave and lap. No bird to call. No insect to buzz.

Winter can be like that. Nothing but the sheer sound of silence. We stood in the quiet. Our clothes steamed nicely in the late morning sun. Our breath left tell-tale plumes of exhaust. Only the internal beat of hearts intent on hiking hinted at movement.

The land frozen in solitude, the sun unable to break through despite its brilliance. It was good for us to be there. We could have pitched a tent and remained forever. To move on would have meant the shattering of silence, the return to the din of quotidian life.

Our lives are, for the most part, busy. We're about many things – raising children, waging war, healing the sick, earning a living … making our mark. And make our mark we must. But there comes a time in every life when other priorities call for attention. We've raised our children, made our million, maybe even saved a soul or two. Still, there eventually comes a day when the hubbub of life needs to take a turn, let us say, inward.

Making our outward mark on the world. That's relatively easy and is bolstered by youth and energy, when we're, as John Steinbeck noted in his novel *The Grapes of Wrath*, "full a piss n' vinegar."

But, live long enough, let our bodies fall into the disrepair of longevity, and we come face to face with another need. I call it the need for silence, or solitude, or to use a more philosophical turn of phrase, the need to "turn inward to oneself."

We may have been blessed, or just plain lucky, to have practised the art of silence from our early years. A regular practice of prayer and meditation may have engendered that silence. Or care for others or joy in the gift of creation. Or simply the regular practice of reading good literature. Count your blessings if that happened to you. Most of us may not have been so fortunate. Fear not, however. The angels of God know never to give up. Eventually, you will be led into the silence of the desert. Even Jesus Christ could not escape this path of humanity.

In the silence of life, you will meet a new person. Sometimes this encounter is rough, and even bloody. Either way, it's painful. Why? Because we never wish, as an old dog, to learn new tricks.

It's a new and wondrous path that we then seek in the silence of the twilight years. Just as we enter the hinterland of the wilderness to seek silence, it is only in the hinterland of our soul that we are blessed with silence. There we encounter a new person, a "new creation," of which Scripture spoke (2 Corinthians 5:17).

You may meet a person with less need to accumulate, to make a mark, to speak many words. You may meet a person who seeks consolation in the simple joys of life. You may come to meet a person who longs more for silence.

Be attentive. You're not going crazy.

On that winter's day in Algonquin Park, we listened long into the silence. Pure, simple, inviting, it called us to listen to the thump of our heart, the precious breath of our lungs, the "given-ness" of creation all around. But, life being what it is, we had to move on. Hopefully, we resumed our path intent on the silence that awaited us at the next turn and bend in the trail.

Brook Trout and Nuclear Apocalypse

Cormac McCarthy is a well-known American writer. You may know him by his celebrated Border Trilogy (*All the Pretty Horses*, 1992; *The Crossing,* 1994; and *Cities of the Plain*, 1998). I know him best as the Pulitzer Prize–winning author of *The Road,* 2006, made into a 2009 film of the same name.

In a post-apocalyptic setting, a man and his son wander a barren world of ash and leaden skies. Marauding gangs of desperate, violent men seek to kill whatever lives. Cannibalism abounds. It's a cold, stark read. I simply loved it.

Page after page carries one forth into the dream of hope in desperate times.

The story ends with a paragraph that surprises. Only here at the end, after a couple of hundred pages and thousands of words, are we introduced to colour. In several magnificent lines of prose, he describes in vivid, intimate detail the muscular and polished bodies of brilliantly coloured brook trout in cold mountain streams. His limpid prose captured my imagination.

Lifting from the page, the words transported me to days gone by, to the smell and feel and swim of trout.

I knew so well of what he spoke. Trout were imprinted on my DNA. I grew up skirting the myriad of ponds and streams of Newfoundland with fly rod in hand. I think I could fly-cast for trout before I could walk. I got it from my dad, and it has never left me. Cormac's words enriched my senses that smelled the mossy trout, eyed their brilliant flash of rose and white in the river channels, felt their tug and pull on my taut, vibrating lines.

Cormack's parting lines continue to haunt me. He describes what is no more in his novel's post-apocalyptic world. A lament for what was lost – brook trout, mountain streams, the hum and mystery of life. A lament for what could never be put back together again.

What took eons to create we can blindly snuff out in seconds – deaden life and chill the air.

No technique of ours will ever put it back. What lament we must bear.

But Cormac's final words are not a call to despair. Love deeply the other and you will never forget to care – care for yourself, for each other, and for the trout-filled mountain streams of this world.

FEBRUARY

Feelings Are Fickle

D o you ever get to the point where what is supposed to be simple becomes a burden? I can feel that way from time to time.

I remember once having finished teaching a three-hour evening class after several days of preparation. It was late. I was weary. I needed to go to bed. But a deadline loomed for the next day. To stay awake in front of a computer screen and work on a project was the last thing I needed. But remain I did.

Be attentive to your feelings, says St. Ignatius. Feelings are the gateway to God. Look to the inner soul to find the mind of God. On the other hand, feelings are fickle. Now this, now that – they can bounce about like liquid fat in a fire. Fizzled feelings, frenzied feelings looking for a place to rest like demons among the pigs.

And so, I can't give much stock to my current feelings. They generally get me nowhere. If I conducted my life according to my feelings, I'd probably be in a bad state of affairs.

I remember my mother advising me when I felt less than inclined to leave the house to attend this or that: "When you get there, you'll feel all right." Not what I wanted to hear, but true nonetheless. Out I would venture, huddled against the night, off to my agreed upon rendezvous. And, sure enough, when I got there, things did work out, invariably so. Mothers have this wisdom, I suppose.

In life, we end up doing a lot of things we least expect. As a rather itinerant Jesuit, I can attest to that. Would I ever have imagined that one day I would be doing this or that? Not on your life. I had other things marked out. I was a man on the move with places to go and things to do.

But, as way leads on to way, we eventually find ourselves in places and with people we sometimes least expect. I used to think that life could be marked out precisely, given enough preparation and skillful reconnaissance.

There finally comes a day when what we once thought important, if not essential, becomes less important and less essential. We enter a moment – or a time of crisis. Familiar moorings shift, the channel of life changes and we find ourselves adrift amid a meandering delta.

A river without any banks doesn't go anywhere. That's a problem for those years when we need goals and objectives. But eventually those fast-moving streams slicing down from the mountains reach the flat deltas of the lowlands. Gone is the flash of clear, fast, crisp water. It is replaced by the warm, slow murky waters of the delta, which are unsure of their direction.

Unknown is the wide-open expanse of the ocean that welcomes the waters. Maybe we need those times of life when clear, well-defined categories no longer work. Ideas of faith, God, self, other. They just don't seem to compute. We lament the loss of crispness and clarity.

But it's only the quiet waters of the delta that can lay down the rich soil. The early mountainous waters don't build up, they simply erode. They have no time for depth or serenity. Only now, far away from the windy, craggy peaks, can the waters take their time, slow a piece, and lay down that rich sediment that builds up.

It's still late. I still want to sleep, but maybe the waters have slowed down just enough that I can sit, take keyboard in hand

and write. Feelings have ceased to matter. Commitment takes over. Don't worry, you'll feel better when you get there. That's true.

I'm now finished – no worse for wear.

Hearts Both Frightened and Free

My heart is best described as both frightened and free. I am never fully there, in the Spirit, so to speak. It's not for lack of effort or will. It just seems to be that way. No matter what, no matter the abundance of grace and joy that may fill my heart, I am fully aware that I don't have it all together. I never will. I need God. I need others.

Maybe that's a good thing. It keeps me honest, grounded, constantly aware that all is grace – even when it doesn't feel so gracious.

They say that fear, not hatred, is the opposite of love. It's fear that tempts us to seek solace in all the wrong places. We call such places "sin." Sin attempts to fill the void of our fearful hearts. Fear creates that gap in the heart. When fear steps in, faith, hope and love exit.

The forms of fear are legion. What will people think of me? Why can't I be as good and generous as others? What if I don't come out on top? What will happen if I fail?

These questions – and many more like them – disturb our peace, sucking dry the springs of living water. Our souls curl up, becoming tepid, worried and distracted. We seek out that which will give solace – immediate solace.

What we find will often remove the sting of daily living. It dulls our senses, becomes an opiate that carries us off into another world, an unreal world. Life doesn't seem so cold or so fearsome anymore. But, in the end, as the drug of sin wears off, we find ourselves back in the same place or, as is often the case, in a worse place. The fears return with a greater vengeance. And the cycle continues.

I wonder if we could define sin as seeking the good in all the wrong places. We seek peace knowing that our hearts are restless. We seek consummation knowing that so much is never fully realized.

Maybe the good reader will protest that I make too little of sin. Maybe you think that I am too soft on sin, trying to explain it away, rationalize our behaviour. Maybe. However, I know from my own life that our hearts are indeed restless. We're complicated. And we can get into some fine mix-ups.

We are all tempted. We all have our places of restlessness with which we struggle. And we all have sinful dispositions that kick in when we become tired and afraid. These are the weeds among the wheat. We will never successfully uproot all the weeds. That would pull up the good wheat as well. The trick is to be aware of the chinks in our armour of love, the weak spots in our castles of life. It is at those weakest spots that the enemy of our human nature will muster all his force to enter our soul.

Be aware. Keep awake. Keep your lamps burning. All this to say that we must guard against our existential fears. These have the potential to become our weak spots, the entry point of the Evil One, who will, as Jesus says, enter like a thief in the night. Stay awake, then. For you know neither the hour nor the day.

Watch out as You Draw Closer to God

The closer you get to God, the more difficult your spiritual life will become. That may sound strange, especially when we assume that being close to God means a well-ordered and happy life.

There's great resistance as we grow closer to God. Our ego seems to gain strength as it realizes the great struggle it faces. It won't give up or lessen its grip without a fight.

St. John of the Cross (1542–1591), Carmelite, mystic, doctor of the Church, understood the meaning of what he termed "darkness" – that struggle of the human soul on its journey to God.

St. John wrote of getting close to God. The closer we get to God, the more we have to let go, to let God be. That may be relatively easy in the early stages, as we convert from a path hell-bent on destruction to a Spirit-led path. But as we progress in the spiritual life, the path of enlightenment grows increasingly difficult. In fact, it may seem at times that complete darkness has descended and all progress is hopeless.

The "way of the flesh" won't give up. It gets harder and harder to free ourselves from our fear and sin. The fear of self-annihilation grows only too strong. Jesus said that unless we die to ourselves, we can never enter the Kingdom of God.

But the self does not want to die: that's the problem. What would we become if we let ourselves fall completely into the mystery of God? To step out into the deep, to let go as we hang precipitously from the cliff edge – such acts of faith are never easy. But we know that this is the only way to freedom.

To live our days not knowing what tomorrow will bring. To forgive when anger and resentment dominate our every thought. To wait in patient faith, unsure of what is happening to us. To speak a word of hope when all live in despair. In a word – to die to ourselves.

This death, this "night of the soul" is intrinsic to the spiritual life. As John of the Cross wrote in *Dark Night of the Soul*, "O, night that guided me. O, night more lovely than the dawn." Maybe Blessed John Henry Newman (1801–1890) had the same experience when he wrote in his 1833 poem "The Pillar of the Cloud,"

> Lead, Kindly Light, amid the encircling gloom
> Lead Thou me on!
> The night is dark, and I am far from home—
> Lead Thou me on!

The "night" is central to the life of the Spirit. The way of the cross is a stepping forth into the mists of darkness. Our inner life must be seared by the piercing fire of God's love that burns through all that separates us from creation, from ourselves and from God. True love will emerge only when tested in the crucible of God's love. His love crucifies our resistance and prepares our minds and hearts for resurrection.

Surprise at Starbucks

I knew they could be crafty and wily, even intelligent, as some are wont to say. But I hadn't expected this sort of behaviour. Off the ground he lifted the soiled Starbucks coffee cup, turned it over with a deft move of his head, and out they poured. They jingled and jangled across the concrete, spilling this way and that.

Tossing the cup aside, the crow pecked and twisted a few coins, heads to tails and tails to heads. Finding nothing of interest, off he trotted and finally flitted away.

As I said, crows can be crafty and wily, but I never thought I'd see one rifle through a panhandler's meagre offerings.

A man has found a home on a cement corner next to Starbucks. I've seen him a few times, huddled asleep in his corner as I pick up an early morning latte on my way somewhere. Today, his street blanket was empty. Off somewhere, I guessed, leaving his cup of coins – a prime target for a pillaging crow.

The Gospel of Luke tells of a poor man named Lazarus who longed to satisfy his hunger with what fell from a rich man's table (Luke 16:19-31). Even the dogs would come and lick his sores, Luke tells us.

In Vancouver, there was a poor man who longed to fill his cup with what fell from the hands of the passers-by. Even the crows would come and attempt to steal, or at least disrupt, what little he had.

Luke goes on to tell us that the poor man died and was carried away by the angels to be with Abraham. The rich man also died – and ended up in Hades in a life of torment and agony.

I entered Starbucks and bought my café latte. Exiting, I saw that the blanket was still empty. The few coins still lay strewn across the concrete, the crow nowhere to be seen.

I moved on, intent on my next destination. But I couldn't move in the same way. An empty blanket, crow-tossed coins, a Starbucks cup on its side … and the echoes of St. Luke ringing in my ears.

The Blind and the Sighted

During a recent walk back from Jericho Beach in Vancouver, I came upon a blind woman. Cane in hand, she veered her way up the sidewalk in front of me. Despite the back-and-forth movement of the cane, her feet knew their way. It was obvious she had travelled this way before.

As I approached, she bent over to the side and stopped. Not used to such a fast approach, I thought. I gave her space, acknowledged her in silence and continued on my way.

Then something happened.

I knew where he was going. His eyes were intent, looking into the distance. He's going to her, I thought. Slowing my pace, I turned to see. Sure enough, his arm reached out, she took it in hers, and linked, they walked ahead.

Up the sidewalk they paced, the blind and the sighted. I turned and continued on my way. I had things to do.

Eventually, I turned again – and stopped this time. The couple were crossing the busy street with the light. All the world had stopped, it seemed. Only the blind and the sighted moved across the pavement, down the sidewalk several metres to a set of stairs. At the foot of the stairs, the couple let each other go, and the blind woman inched up the concrete steps to home.

I turned again, and continued my way up the hill. I did not look back this time. There was nothing more to see. A moment in time, finished, over with, witnessed by only a few. Maybe I was the only one who saw it all – the coupling of the blind and the sighted, the journey together, the letting go when danger had passed.

It was accomplished. But some things linger. Lingering were my thoughts of being too busy and intent on things personal to offer my arm to the blind woman. I knew not her destination, while the crossing guard attendant had obviously known her. Or so I assumed.

What could I have done? Invited myself into the life of the blind? Imagine that. As I walked on, I couldn't shake the thought of my single-mindedness. Sure, I had things to do, meetings to attend, places to go. But such excuses did not satisfy. Like it or not, I had walked by on my busy way.

These feelings of mine may linger for a little while, but they will pass. Thankfully, certain things are eternal – like the image of the blind and the sighted arm in arm. Let those who have eyes see.

MARCH

The Fragrance of God

I somehow figured that the prophet Isaiah was a forester – or at least a bit of a tree hugger.

What else could I think when I heard this reading from Isaiah: "I will put in the wilderness the cedar, the acacia, the myrtle, and the olive; I will set in the desert the cypress, the plane and the pine together, so that all may consider and understand, that the hand of the Lord has done this, the Holy One of Israel has created it" (Isaiah 41:19-20).

When I heard this passage proclaimed, I rejoiced in the fragrance of God. These trees of Isaiah are fragrant trees. How often I associate different forests and tree species with various fragrances. I remember well filling my senses with the fragrance of pine needles warmed by dry, arid winds of interior British Columbia, or the earthy, pungent odours rising from the freshly drenched humid forest floor carpeting the northern boreal forests of Labrador, or the evocative, dizzying colognes emanating from a linden tree in full bloom in the Vosges forests of eastern France. This is the voice of God: ripe, fresh, volatile … Let anyone with a nose smell!

Ad Orientem

With my back to St. Peter's Basilica and my face to the east, I waited in anticipation. The verdant slopes of the Central

Apennines to the east of Rome waited in shadow. The skies shimmered in hues of pink and red.

I'm a morning person. Mornings are pregnant with anticipation. The night has passed and a new day has dawned. What will happen is unknown. That's why morning prayer is best for me. Prayer is, by nature, a dawning affair. It hopes and longs and seeks into the future. Thankful for the past and the present, it leans into the unknown, dependent on the mercy and consolation of God. Prayer begs for the joy of God's Spirit. Only then can decisions be made; only then can the road ahead be seen with greater clarity.

There is a long Christian tradition of *ad orientem*: of building churches that faced east. Priest and people were to face east in their prayer and worship.

Behind me, St. Peter's, aglow in the rising sun, faces east. With its back to the west, it seeks out the eastern dawn each and every day. Night has a limit. Each dawning day witnesses to possibility, to newness of life. Good Friday must eventually give way to Easter Sunday. Our tears will one day be wiped away. The dead will rise, the sick will be healed, the lame will walk, and our spears shall be transformed into ploughshares.

We never know what each day may bring. For some of us it may well be our last day on earth. For others, it's only the beginning. Death and birth, strength and decline, health and sickness, joy and sadness, the new day witnesses our comings and goings.

I like the cosmic focus of our liturgy. Bread and wine, simple gifts of the earth, become divine food for the journey, the Body and Blood of Christ. The waters from the heavens bless and baptize. In our Eucharistic Prayers, we call on the Trinity, who gives life to all things and make them holy.

In his 2003 encyclical *Ecclesia de Eucharistia*, St. John Paul II (1920–2005) assured us of this when he wrote that "the Eucharist is always in some way celebrated *on the altar of the world*. It unites heaven and earth. It embraces and permeates all creation. The Son of God became man in order to restore all creation, in one great act of praise, to the One who made it from nothing" (no. 8).

Our prayer is thus one great act of cosmic love. In the liturgy, nothing should ever be lost.

As I sat silently facing the dawning sun, I sensed the day anew. Our lives are not simply one damn thing after another. There's a freshness ever anew with each day. Rest awhile in the gaze of the east, do it on a regular basis, and the world will never be the same. From the rising of the sun to its setting, may we never presume our days. They're too precious for that.

Let There Be Life

"Precisely how life began is still a mystery ...." Thus did the plant biologist Karl Niklas write in his 2016 book *Plant Evolution: An Introduction to the History of Life.*

I like such honest statements. It's no wonder the writers of Sacred Scripture and most Indigenous peoples around the world had to resort to the use of myth to try and make sense of the very fact of creation. Why is there something rather than nothing? Why is there life rather than non-life? In fact, why is there anything at all?

Apparently, the newborn Earth was by no means a welcoming place for life, at least life as we have come to know it. The so-called Hadean period of the embryonic Earth was hostile to life. A molten rock surface – devoid of atmosphere, radiated by the sun's deadly ultraviolet rays, bombarded by the rocky debris of a nascent solar system – provided little incentive for life.

But life's urgings could not be stopped. Out of the hell of Hades, life would emerge.

Niklas outlines four stages as precursors to the miracle of life:

1. The creation of abiotically synthesized small organic molecules such as amino acids and nucleotides, the building blocks of what would become life.

2. The joining of these small molecules into larger polymers such as proteins, lipids and nucleic acids.

3. The creation of the hereditary molecules of life: ribonucleic acid (RNA) and deoxyribonucleic acid (DNA).

4. The aggregation of these abiotically synthesized molecules into the rudiments of cell-like structures that had an internal biochemical and biophysical environment different from that found on the exterior of the cell-like structures.

At the end of Earth's Hadean period, the atmosphere and the oceans began to stabilize. Such relative stability permitted the beginnings of life. The oldest known terrestrial rocks, found in northern Quebec, date from around 4.3 billion years ago. The oldest known life forms date back 3.6 million years or so. Here we define life as having the ability to process energy and matter in ways that permit reproduction, growth and survival.

Next would come the greatest of life's revolutions with photosynthesis, when life gained the amazing ability to convert the abundant light energy of the sun into chemical or food energy. The by-product of photosynthesis, oxygen gas, would eventually accumulate to such an extent that the atmosphere itself would change from an oxygen-poor to an oxygen-rich one, permitting the flourishing of a whole new suite of life forms, including, eventually, you and me.

We know the theoretical, indeed possible, outline of how life developed once it came on the scene. But as for how abiotic or non-life molecular entities became biotic life forms – well, that's another story.

In the Nicene Creed, we proclaim belief "in the Holy Spirit, the Lord, the giver of life." In John's Gospel, Jesus is quoted as saying, "I came that they may have life, and have it abundantly" (John 10:10). Christian inertia is an inertia towards life.

So far, the origin of biological life is still a mystery. Eventually, we may come to unlock the biochemical and biophysical steps that lead to life. But even then, wondrous as such knowledge will be, we will be forever faced with the wonder of life itself. Cherish life. Cherish what simply is. It's a wonder to behold, even if for now we know not its origin.

Sex and the Foot of the Cross

We don't normally conjoin sex and the cross of Christ. Yet there is often no better place to reflect on our sexuality than at the foot of the cross.

We don't necessarily define ourselves by our sexuality, but there's no doubt that there may be nothing more powerful in our lives. It's so hot that often we dare not touch it. Someone may be hot, hot, hot … but our sexuality is surely never cold, cold, cold.

When we think of morality, we often think of sexual morality. Much of Catholic moral teaching centres on personal sexual morality. Think of the internet, and one of the first things that comes to mind may be pornography. Sex is best done in private, yet we are aware of our sexualized public space.

I recently attended an event during which several men and women – some married, some single, some gay, some straight – shared their struggles with affectivity and sexuality. It was a holy event.

With candour, honesty, humility – and not a little trepidation, I am sure, did these people share their struggles. Hi, my name is Jane Doe and "I slept with whomever I could, man or woman, it didn't matter." Hi, my name is John Doe, and "I struggle with internet pornography and masturbation."

As I said, it was a holy event. I couldn't help thinking of the biblical woman with the irregular flow of blood. "If I only touch his cloak, I will be made well" (Matthew 9:21). And she was made well.

We all need to touch the hem of the cloak of Jesus, particularly in terms of our sexuality. Our sexuality is simply so powerful. It has the power to heal – and the power to scar.

Sex can be the source of life and love. By that very fact, our sexuality is sacred: it is of God. Sex can also be the source of great harm and shame. A touch of avarice replaces a touch of love. Lovemaking transforms into rape. Sexual abuse confuses us deeply and we struggle with the after-effects. Give our bodies and bed to another too quickly and we wonder what went wrong.

There's power in our bodies. We are not simply body and soul or soul and body, but rather embodied spirits and spirited bodies. Mingle our bodies – and our hearts and souls fuse – or confuse. Pay attention to creation, to our bodies, to the stuff of matter. That's where our hearts and souls find peace – or confusion.

Jesus professed that he had come to give us life – and life to the full. He became body, flesh and blood, so that our bodies may become holy. And holy they are. The mystery of the Incarnation proclaims that loud and clear.

In our sexuality, the greatest gift we can give ourselves is a spirit of gentleness. Be gentle with yourself. Our sexuality is never fully understood. It can only be comprehended at the foot of the cross. Be attentive to its power. It's a God-given divine power. It's meant to save and to heal. Bow your heads and bend your knee. That is all we can do before this sacred fire of God's

Love. Therefore, treat it gently, love it fully and share it in ways that truly give life.

A Fast for Nature

I didn't expect it would last this long. I knew I would experience some adjustments, but I had no idea it would be this difficult. The daily diarrhea finally broke after (excuse the pun), a solid week. Not too bad an adjustment, I thought, after a 44-day water and juice fast.

Several Lents ago, I did something new. From Ash Wednesday until sundown on Holy Thursday I fasted. For a period of 44 days, I took only water, and fruit and vegetable juice. No solid food touched my lips. Before the fast, a glass of V-8 juice would have been the farthest thing from my mind. During the fast, it became a regular companion.

Why such a fast? My being middle aged may have had something to do with it – a desire to break forth, out of the routine, into something bold. A Catholic version of red convertible syndrome. No, it was simpler than that. I wanted to witness, in a public way, to the sacredness of creation.

I had been thinking of such a public act for several years. For some time, I had been involved in environmental protection and preservation – with little or no effect. The fast would be a witness to the beauty and glory of God in creation. In hindsight, maybe the fast was more importantly an attempt to save my own soul. My efforts at ecological care had somehow permitted frustration, cynicism and even anger to enter my heart. I needed conversion.

So, when I awoke on Ash Wednesday, I knew what I would do. I would fast for nature. It would be a public fast as well, with press releases and the hope of media engagement. A private fast, paradoxically, risked the danger of becoming too narcissistic, too self-absorbed. It had to be public. My inner scape needed to express itself in landscape.

We could define the sacred as that which is most important to us, that which leads to life, beauty and community. For me, nature served that purpose, and therefore was sacred. More importantly, creation was of God, and therefore was sacred in and of itself.

My interior lament had to find expression. Before the seemingly unstoppable hemorrhaging of beauty and life by our destructive forces, I needed to find a voice.

The hunger pangs disappeared after three or four days, followed by days of relative peace. But that, too, would disappear as the fast continued amid my work and travel. Some days were better than others. I became anxious. Maybe it was simply my body consuming itself: first the fat reserves (of which there were little to start with) and then the protein. That can cause the mind to wonder, no doubt.

I was adamant that the fast not be construed as a hunger strike or an act rooted in self-righteous anger. For that reason, the holy season of Lent had to be the boundaries for my fast. Lent gave it a beginning and an end. It was not a hunger strike. I did not wish to publicly shame the government. It was to be a Lenten time of prayer and fasting. I longed for a new heaven and a new earth, for that rainbow in the sky that connected earth and heaven after the cleansing waters of the flood. And in the midst of it all, I longed for my own conversion of soul and mind.

Lent is a time that opens space for change. Did the fast change government policy on protected areas and land use policy? Not in the least, I think. Did the fast open public space for a wider conversation? In a limited way, yes. Did the fast change me? Most definitely. Personally, the fast has strengthened the conviction of my work for the protection of wild lands in Canada.

St. Ignatius claimed that love is expressed better in deeds than in words. For me, the fast was an act of faith, hope and love. In a word, the fast became a prayer.

Three to four weeks into the fast, I had to diminish my daily brisk walk. I maintained my regular work with the Newfoundland and Labrador Wildlife Division, pastoral work on the weekends and daily exercise. The English Carmelite Ruth Burrows focused my spiritual reading. Before the fast ended, I would have to stop what I was doing to conserve energy. Pounds were melting away as my body turned to the fat and eventually protein reserves for sustenance. Deep into the fast, most days were fine, but increasingly I experienced bad days characterized by a "*je ne sais quoi*," an anxious malaise that dominated the hours. A growing hunger, no doubt. Or the unrest and disquiet of my body eating into itself. The final week of the fast found me drawn and tired.

Growing up in eastern Newfoundland, I was seduced by the beauty and vitality of the forests, bogs and barrens, the vigour and freshness of the North Atlantic. The love affair continues. The fast only consummated the love in these middle years of my life.

Particularly heartening for me were the words and letters of support and encouragement from family, friends, colleagues and brother Jesuits. Letters from people I have never met, encouraging me on the way.

A few days into the fast, I witnessed from my window out across the bay a double rainbow. I reached for my bible and read aloud the cosmic covenant in the book of Genesis: "I have set my bow in the clouds, and it shall be a sign of the covenant between me and the earth" (Genesis 9:13).

I wept. The rainbow dissipated. I knew I had taken the right path.

The creation of God is sacred. It is holy and the womb of our salvation.

APRIL

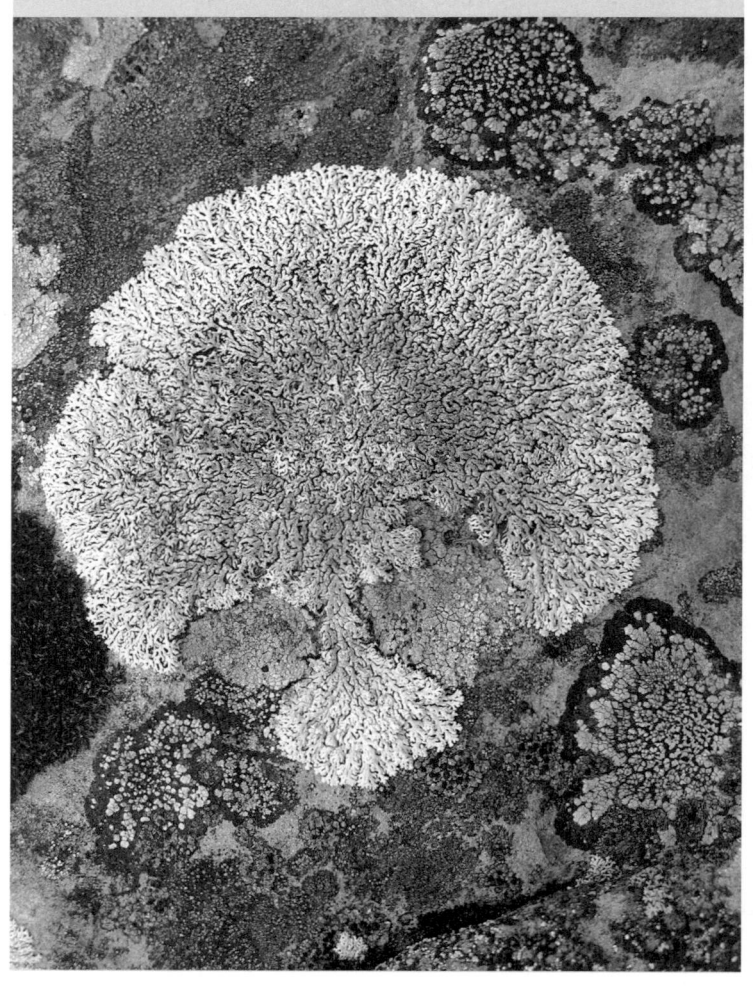

A Cemetery at Easter

I love walking through graveyards – they're so life-giving. One of my favourite Toronto walks through the city's forested ravines leads me to Mount Pleasant cemetery. Founded in 1876, the 81-hectare cemetery is filled with extensive walking paths through gorgeous rolling parkland covered with exquisite art and monuments and featuring handsome, mature trees of many species. For me, the cemetery has become a sanctuary of quiet and contemplation amid the rush and roar of civic life.

A lush growth of lichens on base-rich limestone monuments witnesses the gentle passage of time.

What impresses me most, I think, are the varied and creative inscriptions left by the living – many of whom now rest in eternity themselves, I imagine.

On every headstone, sentiments of love and memory capture one's attention. No doubt crafted in grief and sadness, the timeless words now speak somehow of hope and joy. Inert tombstones witness to the vitality of faith, hope and love, three things that last forever, as St. Paul reminds us (1 Corinthians 13:13). The headstones will eventually fade away, even those made of granite, but love will remain forever. That's what cemeteries celebrate. That's what cemeteries witness.

Every day that I walk back and forth to work along the busy Toronto streets of Bloor and Bay, I pass many people. Sometimes I wonder what they believe – about life, about death, about love, about sadness and grief. I ask myself the same questions. I walk as a member of that bustling crowd.

Spring has sprung, days are lengthening, the world is greening and growing. On Easter, we celebrate life, that mystery that never ceases to amaze.

So pervasive is the universe's quest for life that one day the molecular precursors would gather and self-replicate, would unify and complexify, would cooperate and celebrate. Shrouded in timeless mystery, the beginnings of life would one day so love each other that the greatest novelty of all would appear – the emergence of consciousness. The universe would discover its own beautiful wonder in and through the mystery of the human mind.

During Easter we witness that Life is the final Word of the universe. Death, though ever so obvious, is never and can never be the final word. Death and destruction are real, often terribly and painfully so, but they are only the paths to resurrection and re-creation.

At the heart of Easter is Life. No wonder the Easter bunny and the Easter egg have become secular symbols of Easter. Both are signs of fertility and new life. But the most telling symbol for us is the cross. A paradoxical image, where an instrument of death and evil is transformed into the Tree of Glory.

No tomb, no defeat, no failure can mark us forever. They will have their day. Live long enough and you will have to walk through the Red Sea, you will have to cross the barren desert, but remember: The Promised Land beckons.

On Easter Sunday, the most holy of days, celebrate the fact that you live, that you have been blessed with breath for another day. Christ is indeed risen. All of creation rises in Christ. Your heartache and worry rises in Christ. Live this day. Truly live this day.

A blessed and holy Easter to all – today and every day.

A Lesson Learned

Once upon a time, I attended mass at St. Peter the Fisherman, a small mission church in the quiet hamlet of Cherryfield, about 30 minutes from where I was staying in northern Maine. It seemed that everyone knew each other, as is understandable in a country parish. The pastor, a man in his 60s, rather unkempt, collar undone, with a belt loop that needed repair, greeted his flock with ease and warmth. Opening announcements included a call for someone to cut the grass around the church and for donations to the parish food bank. A community spirit was evident.

As the pastor began his homily, I groaned interiorly. Oh, no, not again. Not another diatribe about the new Roman Missal translation. Hadn't enough been said? Let's move forward.

He opened his homily by noting that many people considered aspects of the new translation to be somewhat archaic. Sure, I thought, we all know that, but in the grand scheme of things, it seemed a minor matter compared to the grave challenges faced by millions of people each day. Why continue to harp on such trivial matters?

The pastor focused on the replacement of the word "cup" with the word "chalice" in the Eucharistic Prayer. For decades, we have said that Jesus took the cup, gave thanks, gave it to his disciples and said … You know the rest. Now, the priest must say that Jesus took the *chalice*, gave thanks, gave it to his disciples ….

When the new translation of the Roman Missal first appeared, I was somewhat irritated with the replacement of the word "cup" by what I thought to be the much more "liturgical" word "chalice." Much of what I had read, and my discomfort with proclaiming that Jesus died for "the many" rather than "for all," had not disposed me to accept "chalice" for "cup." I had associated such changes with a somewhat overall retrograde spirit exemplified by the new translation.

The pastor's homily proved me naive and wrong. He went on to explain the difference between a cup and a chalice. With a good use of props, Father Gene noted that a cup is a relatively deep and narrow receptacle meant for one person, whereas a chalice is shallow and wide and meant for communal drinking.

Jesus would therefore have passed among his disciples a chalice and not a cup. The chalice of blessing was meant for all. All were to take and drink of the one chalice filled with the blood of the new and eternal covenant.

I had obviously come to accept the use of the term "chalice" in the Eucharistic Prayer before hearing this homily. But I don't think I had fully understood the translator's intent in replacing "cup" with "chalice." To be sure, I like to think I had always appreciated the full communal spirituality of the Eucharist. But when it came to the name change, I seemed to have missed something.

Sometimes, you think you know. But, often, our blinders are too hidden for us to see. Our natural reflexes can act too quickly. We are often blind. Maybe that's why Jesus talked so much of the hardened heart that is blind – while those many considered to be blind can actually see.

It's difficult to be reminded of one's blind spots at times. But, that's pure grace. Grace that can come winging in from left field – even in a small country church in the middle of a field in the woods of northern Maine. I thank Father Gene for a lesson learned.

The Ecological Crisis:
Science and Faith in Dialogue

There exists only one world. As such, both scientific and theological/spiritual language have a rightful role to play in understanding that one world. As St. John Paul II expressed in his 1988 letter to the Director of the Vatican Observatory, "Science can purify religion from error and superstition; religion can purify science from idolatry and false absolutes. Each can draw the other into a wider world, a world in which both can flourish."

In our current eco-crisis, we need both science and faith. Scientists need to hear from theologians, and theologians need to hear from scientists. Where once religious language (such as in the book of Genesis) and traditions were cited as the cause of the environmental crisis, many now realize that we fail to address the ecological crisis adequately without religious language.

Science, as well as technology, economics and politics, is necessary, but never sufficient. People's care for nature is based not on facts, either scientific or economic, but rather on values or principles. Scientific understanding will necessarily inform our decision making, but it can never decide for us what constitutes the good. Only religious language can do that.

The ecological crisis is not, first and foremost, a scientific or economic or technological crisis. It is, rather, a moral crisis, a cultural crisis, a spiritual crisis. It speaks to our most deeply held values regarding the created world and our sense of our place in that world. John Zizioulas, the influential Orthodox Christian theologian, noted in a 1989–1990 series of lectures on ecology and theology that what we need is "not an ethic, but an ethos. Not a programme, but an attitude and a mentality. Not a legislation, but a culture." Former Oxford University geographer Michael Williams (1935–2009) put it more bluntly when, at the end of his 1998 magnum opus, *Deforesting the Earth*, he affirmed that "unless forests ... are regarded as 'sacred' in some way or another ... sustainability of the forest will continue to diminish." In other words, we need religious language that speaks to the possibility of conversion, or *metanoia*.

Only religious discourse can offer what is needed to meet the ecological challenge. Whether we seek a new morality, a new culture or a sense of the deeply personal and sacred order of creation, we are longing for what only religion can provide. Authentic religion invites us to contemplation before creation, to a holy vision that embraces the fullness of God's creation, to a personal and social conversion, to a dying to ourselves so that all creation may live and flourish. We seek a re-enchantment of nature as the Word and Beauty of God.

It may only be as contemplatives, as mystics conformed by grace to Christ, that we will have eyes to see and ears to hear the call of God to fullness of life. "I came that they may have life, and have it abundantly" (John 10:10). "I call heaven and earth to witness against you today that I have set before you life and death, blessings and curses. Choose life so that you and your descendants may live" (Deuteronomy 30:19). Yes, life to the full, for the greater glory of God.

Of Harp Seals and Earth Day

I write on Earth Day after having received an email from a friend and colleague in Newfoundland. He just returned from the annual harp seal hunt. He and his crew took 851 seals. Apparently, the sea ice was scarce this year.

My friend is a fisher on Newfoundland's Great Northern Peninsula. Each spring, the sea ice rides the cold Labrador Current south, squeezing through the Strait of Belle Isle narrows into the northern reaches of the Gulf of St. Lawrence. And each year, my friend and other fishers of this region go out onto the sea ice in search of the harp seal.

I have witnessed the majesty of the spring ice off the Great Northern Peninsula. As far as the eye can see, across to the distant shores of Quebec, lies mile after mile of sea ice, brilliant and tortuous under the warming spring sun. But the ice is not alone. Thousands of harp seals make their journey south with the pack ice that acts as a nursery for the birth of the baby whitecoats, so named because of their shiny white fur that is transformed after several moults into the harp-marked grey pelt of the adults.

The hunting of the harp seal has engendered a significant amount of protest. Pamela Anderson, Sir Paul McCartney and Brigitte Bardot have been but a few of the many celebrities who have opposed the annual spring seal hunt. Their opinions are shared by many.

I am not as clear as they are. I grew up on baked seal meat and seal flipper pie. Newfoundland has traditionally been a culture of hunters and gatherers. That tradition runs deep in the history and memory of the people, particularly the Inuit and Innu of Labrador.

I have come to view issues like the seal hunt as not simply ecological issues or as not simply economic or cultural issues. They are much more complex than that. We are faced with much broader eco-social or socio-ecological issues that demand great wisdom.

Contemporary understanding acknowledges that any ecological issue must be addressed within the wider dimensions of human institutions, political and economic structures, culture and even spirituality. Sustaining people and ecosystems in a changing world – that is the challenge.

Will we one day decide to no longer hunt the harp seal on the Arctic spring ice? Maybe. Maybe not. Whatever decision is made, hopefully it will be a decision that respects both the integrity of human culture in the North Atlantic and the integrity of this amazing wonder of the natural world.

Creation and Destruction of Life

In 2010, two articles in *Science*, the reputable weekly magazine of the American Association for the Advancement of Science, caught my attention. One article reported the creation of a bacterial cell controlled by an artificially produced genome. The other article reported that the rate of global biodiversity loss does not appear to be slowing.

A 24-person team at the J. Craig Venter Institute in Maryland and California announced a dream. They created from scratch in the lab a complete bacterial genome found in species X. They then transferred this artificial genome into a close relative, bacterial species Y. Lo and behold, they produced new species X cells that are controlled only by the synthetic chromosome. Voilà – artificial life.

The other report, written by a 45-person team from around the world, assessed the 2002 commitment of world leaders (under the 1992 Convention on Biological Diversity) to significantly reduce the rate of global biodiversity loss. Their results are sobering. Most indicators of the state of biodiversity showed declines, whereas the indicators of negative pressures on biodiversity showed increases. In other words, the hemorrhaging of the life of the world continues.

In my ordination card of 1994, I used the following quote from Jesus: "I came that they may have life, and have it abundantly. (John 10:10)." In the Nicene Creed, we profess faith in

"God, the Father … maker of heaven and earth, of all things visible and invisible." Jesus Christ is the one through whom "all things were made." The Holy Spirit is "the Lord, the giver of life." The Trinity is a Trinity of Life.

The juxtaposition of the two scientific reports I mentioned can be disturbing. Artificial life was achieved at great expense, an estimated $40 million US, and effort, with 20 people working for more than a decade at some of the most sophisticated biomedical labs in the world. In one sense, it's an amazing technical accomplishment. On the other hand, it is disconcerting as notions of what life is become fluid. Even the genetic engineers of this cell admit that "as synthetic genomic applications expand, we anticipate that this work will continue to raise philosophical issues that have broad societal and ethical implications." An understatement, to be sure.

The other report documents all too well the decline in the God-given life of the planet. Although the authors did not express it, continued biodiversity loss will also have broad societal and ethical implications.

It used to be that only God could give life and take it away. But we have eaten of the fruit of the tree in the middle of the garden. We have the power to create life, transform life, nurture life, destroy life.

Life – all life: that is the heart of the matter for our faith. Life is at the core of our everlasting covenant with God. God said, "Choose life so that you and your descendants may live" (Deuteronomy 30:19). We have the power. Let us choose well.

MAY

Vision of the Heart

I n what areas have the Jesuits in Canada made progress? In what areas have the Jesuits of Canada suffered declines or danger of declines?

It was with these two basic questions that I began my work as procurator for the Jesuits in English Canada in 2012. My mission was to visit all the Jesuit communities in Canada from St. John's to Vancouver to pose these two questions to Jesuits and our friends and colleagues, and to submit my findings in a report to our Father General (affectionate title for the head of the Society of Jesus) in Rome.

Come the end of June 2012, I joined other elected procurators from all over the world for an eight-day retreat and a week-long meeting with Father General in Nairobi, Kenya. The purpose of this meeting was to assess the state of the international Society of Jesus.

It's always good to self-evaluate. I was never really one for New Year's resolutions or a slavish attention to goal-setting in my life, but ongoing discernment, particularly in the form of the daily Ignatian Examen, is essential for those who desire to grow deeply in the spiritual life.

Socrates is said to have once noted that the unexamined life is not worth living. A wise notion.

The Christian life is just such a venture – or adventure. Let those who have eyes see, and those who have ears hear. Jesus forever reminded his followers and listeners that the key to the life of faith is a discerning heart. "The heart has its reasons of which reason knows nothing," opined the French philosopher Pascal.

The Christian life calls us to develop that third eye, that vision of the heart that invites us to look beyond appearances, to see God in all creation, to witness God in each other, to witness the hand of God in our daily lives.

Seeing God in all things becomes our hope and foundation. That is the rock of faith on which we live. Seeing God in all things, in good times and bad, in sickness and in heath, on the highways – as well as the cul-de-sacs and dead ends of life. God's grace knows no bounds.

Sometimes I may be bewildered or exasperated by life – or enchanted or supported by life. Either way, God has never left me. How to be aware of the abiding presence of God in my fear and hesitancy is the key – and how never to forget God in the euphoria of my delights and successes.

In my role as procurator, I had 15 or more Canadian cities to visit to prepare for our international meeting. I listened to the stories of brother Jesuits and their apostolic partners. I heard stories of growth and success – as well as stories of decline and failure.

But maybe the stories of success and failure will not be the real stories. For, in the end, it's all God's doing, or *opus Dei*. Obviously, we are intimately associated with building the Kingdom of God. But I have come to realize that what we call the Kingdom of God is exactly that – God's Kingdom. It is not our kingdom. Our task is to develop hearts wise enough, minds supple enough and faith courageous enough to read our story in the light of the enduring story of God.

A Mother's Faith, a Mother's Love

A favourite picture is one of myself as a child nestled in the arms of my 26-year-old mother. My Madonna image. I am preoccupied with my small peaked cap, while my mom beams in the photographer's direction. I'm now more than twice as old as my mother was in that photo. Where have the years gone?

My mom's two brothers were alcoholics. Leo, the eldest, succumbed to his drinking at an early age. The Aqua Velva and other alcohol-based substitutes were too much for his body. Her other brother lived a long life – and grew into a holy man. I loved him dearly. He was so proud of my priesthood.

After the birth of each of her four children, Mom was back to work as soon as possible. At one point, young nannies were hired to care for us after school. I think that we four put the nannies to the test at times … like the day when an exasperated nanny called Mom at work to tell her that something terrible had happened. Expecting the worst, Mom hurried home, only to find that we had ceased the rock fight with our neighbours and the head wounds had stopped bleeding.

From time to time, Mom would bring me home a Little Golden Book, very popular during the 1960s of my youth. *Mother Goose*, *The Little Red Hen* and *The Three Bears* were especially endearing. My love for reading and the written word are rooted in those gifts from Mom. I am forever grateful.

I don't seem to remember a whole lot from my youth, but one thing stands out – the nightly ritual of being tucked in by Mom. Everything was right with the world, regardless of what the day had wrought. The fresh, vibrant scent of bedsheets and pillowcases just in from the line (Mom still hangs out her laundry), being tucked in tight under the blankets, Mom leaning over me to kiss me goodnight. Remind me of this if I ever approach senility.

Mom was my first spiritual director or soulmate. That role has not ceased. My failures and hurts, my rebellions and waywardness, my joys and blessings – she has absorbed them all. During it all, she has carried her own struggles and hurts, ecstasies and contentment.

I hope you don't think that my mother had it all together. She didn't, obviously. No one does. But whatever came her way, her profound faith held sway when all else seemed absurd and random. She pondered deeply all that happened. She treasured all things in her heart and invited life into the crucible of prayer. I venture to say that Christ has become her constant companion.

She expressed much of this in writing. One day, she wrote the following in a letter to me: "It is only now that I see a lot of the pain Dad and I had in our childhoods, and perhaps we were both running away from our own situations as opposed to entering a loving relationship. But, despite all the storms, love did bloom and continues to blossom and grow, and please God it will do so for the rest of our days. One thing I will say about marriage is that you must work at it every day of your life. In matters of love, the past is gone, let us learn from it; the future is unknown, let us live in hope; for all we have is today in which to live to our full potential and to 'be still and know that I am God.'"

Words born of faith, words born of life – the life of a mother.

Christian and Muslim Martyrs

On January 4, 2011, Mr. Salman Taseer (1944–2011), a Pakistan politician and businessman and governor of the Pakistan province of Punjab, was assassinated by his bodyguard, shot 26 times.

On March 2, 2011, Mr. Shahbaz Bhatti (1968–2011), Pakistan's federal minister of minority affairs, was assassinated in a hail of bullets as he left his mother's house for a cabinet meeting. The killers identified themselves as members of the Pakistan Taliban and al-Qaeda.

Bhatti was Roman Catholic. Taseer was Muslim. Both publicly opposed their country's blasphemy laws that prescribed death for anyone convicted of insulting the Prophet Mohammed.

Pope Benedict XVI, in his March 7, 2011, Angelus address, stated, "I call on Lord Jesus that the moving sacrifice of the life of Pakistani Minister Shahbaz Bhatti may rekindle in people the courage and commitment to protect religious freedom for all mankind and in this way, also promote equal dignity for all."

Bhatti had received numerous international awards for his tireless efforts as an advocate for human rights and freedom from oppression for all minority peoples. "Jesus is the nucleus of my life," says Bhatti, "and I want to be his true follower through my actions by sharing the love of God with poor, oppressed, victimized, needy and suffering people of Pakistan."

The Pakistan bishops wanted the Church to proclaim Mr. Bhatti as a martyr for the faith. I was sure this would happen, and my hopes were not unfounded: Shahbaz Bhatti was declared a Servant of God in March 2016, five years after his assassination. He is on his way to be declared a saint of the Catholic Church.

But I wondered if something else could happen. What would it mean for the Church to declare both Bhatti *and* Taseer martyrs to the truth of justice, peace and love? Is it possible? How would this be received by Christians – and Muslims? I don't know. I simply had a sense that the world needs the combined witness of these two men. A Muslim and a Christian, a Christian and a Muslim, both of whom died for their belief in the dignity of the human person.

The blood of martyrs is the seed of the Church. Maybe in this case the blood of the martyrs will be the seed of the world, a seed that will take root in the hearts of men and women of goodwill. We need witnesses to interreligious dialogue and to peace.

Did not Jesus himself say that it will not be those who say "Lord, Lord," who will necessarily enter the kingdom of heaven, but only those who hear his words and act on them (Matthew 7:21)?

Bhatti and Taseer, each in their own way, heard the word of the Lord and acted on it. These two sons of Abraham paid for their convictions with their lives. May their blood not have spilled in vain. May their deaths be a light to the nations for all to see.

There's More to Development

I remember a talk given by a minister of natural resources for the Government of Newfoundland and Labrador. He was sharing his perspective on the industrial development potential in Labrador. I heard about mines and dams and offshore oil, about maximization, investment and potential, but curiously, there was something missing. Not one word was uttered about the development and potential of provincial protected areas in Labrador.

The kind reader may respond, "What do you expect from the minister of natural resources? That's not his mandate. Nature is what you dam, mine, drill, cut and net for a profit. That's development."

Developing protected areas. Surely you jest. We all know that protected areas sterilize a landscape. Even a fool understands that protected areas steal jobs and stymie the creation of financial wealth.

Well, not really.

There's another story that is never told – a story of how nature provides much more than food, fibre, fuel or minerals. Nature also generates a vast array of riches that include recreation and ecotourism, and cultural heritage, not to mention spiritual, religious and inspirational values. And of course, let's not forget those basic, indispensable natural "services," such as clean water, fresh air and a non-toxic, life-giving land.

The minister spoke of an important but essentially limited notion of development. Labrador's potential involves more than dams and mines. It also involves a rich array of protected areas.

Economic development includes natural resource development. But it also includes protected areas development. Ask the people of Newfoundland's Great Northern Peninsula about the economic impact of that protected area we call Gros Morne National Park. Ask the United Nations about the vitality of the World Network of Biosphere Reserves that promotes conservation of biological and cultural diversity *and* economic and social development. Believe it or not, protected areas, if properly designed, developed and financed, can create wealth – the full range of wealth that supports authentic, integral human development.

The natural resources minister spun a story of what constitutes development. Maybe he was unable to say much more. But it's a myopic, truncated vision that fails to tell the whole story. We need a wider, deeper, longer and more authentic vision for our future. It's a vision that has been sorely lacking for a long time.

The Tapestry of Life

Not long ago, I gave several public lectures in St. John's, Newfoundland. People whom I had not seen in years came to the different events.

As a Jesuit priest, I live a somewhat peripatetic life – a fancy word for "hobo," I suppose. I move around a lot. Many different missions in many parts of Canada, the United States and even farther afield. I meet people, get to know many people, work with many people and, if luck or chance permit, become friends with some people.

But, as always, I eventually have to move on. It's most often me who seems to do the moving. Others seem much more stationary than me.

I must admit to a certain freedom that comes with the ability to move like that. I am enriched and blessed by the people and places that weave in and out of my life. That's the operative word – weave. I try not to cling or wish for more. I can't. That would be too difficult – and too destructive. How to move along through life and across this earth with a lightness marked by gratitude. That is key for me.

And so, my life is not marked by a permanence or solidity. Rather, it's ephemeral and loose. There's the normal pain that emerges from this migrant life. Getting used to new places has been relatively easy for me. Each place becomes a home for me. But that victory did not come easy or early – not by any means. In the early years, displacement was unsettling and painful. Airports and hotels proved cold and foreign. Happily, that has changed. Don't ask me how. Maybe years of itinerancy and plenty of prayer offered me the grace of dispersion.

As I get on in years, maybe change will once again become more difficult. Maybe not. I'll leave that for later and try not to worry too much about it for now.

The beauty of such an existence has been the slow, steady, sure crafting of a tapestry of life. I have come to see that I don't actually make my life. Rather, life transforms me. People make me. Places make me. And this making or crafting creates something beautiful that is marked by a seemingly infinite tapestry of strands.

People and places and events weave in and out of my life. Friends come and go. Some friends seem to remain forever. The latter are necessarily few, it seems. Some people mark us, albeit for a fleeting moment. They come into our lives, do their magic and, just as swiftly, it seems, they are gone, never to be seen again. Others seem to weave in and out over the years, gently, regularly, like waves on the seashore. Still others crash on our shores with the force and fury of a winter storm.

Through it all, a tapestry is woven. A tapestry of intricacy and colour, of pattern and shape. The amazing thing is that such a tapestry is never finished, it seems. We never see the overall pattern. The weave is never the same consistency, and loose ends may stray here and there: the weave and woof of life creates its mark.

During the recent talks that I gave, people from all parts of my past seemed to emerge, even people from 30 to 40 years ago. We picked up again – seamlessly, it seemed – happy to see each other. How much water has gone under the bridge since last we travelled together? What stories could we share of what had happened in the years that had passed? We may never see each other again. But somehow, another thread had been added to the tapestry of life.

I returned home from the public lectures content, wishful and maybe even a bit nostalgic. But, overall, I ended the days with a deep, abiding sense of wonder and gratitude. Wonder at the myriad of ways people have woven themselves in and out of my life over the years. Grateful for who I have become because of them.

JUNE

The Church Is Who We Are

I n Pope Benedict XVI's 2009 encyclical *Caritas in Veritate*, he stated that the whole Church "in all her being and act-ing ... is engaged in promoting integral human development" (no. 11). He confirms that "authentic human development concerns the whole of the person in every single dimension."

Imagine ... every single dimension. Nothing is to be left out. In other words, absolutely nothing that concerns human-ity is not, at the same time, the concern of the Church. Pope Francis no doubt felt the same way when, on January 1, 2017, he created the brand new Dicastery for Promoting Integral Human Development. According to the Discastery's statutes, it expresses the Holy See's concern for issues of justice and peace, including those related to migration, health, charitable works and the care of creation.

We often think that we live in the world and then go to church. Maybe the Franciscan priest Richard Rohr has a better way of expressing it. We live in the Church, the Body of Christ, and go to the world. Church is not something you attend, but something you are. You don't join the Church, you breathe it.

God so loved the world that he sent his only Son (John 3:16). *So loved the world* – we need a lifetime to plumb the depths of these few words. All the disciplines and faculties of our univer-sities, all the courses and seminars taught and followed, each in their own way attempts to treat of humanity and our world.

However, each discipline can only admit to one vision of what it means to be human. Our challenge is to integrate these many and varied visions so that our full humanity is served.

The Catholic imagination is bold enough to long for authentic human development. Such a venture is not for lazy minds. It will demand a rigorous and honest engagement of humanity's hopes and dreams, failures and fears. A Catholic ghetto narrows the vision of God.

In your learning and teaching and doing, root your intelligence and passion in the Body of Christ, in the world. "I came that they may have life, and have it abundantly" (John 10:10): this was the passion of Christ. You are called to nothing less.

A Father and Fractions

My dad never finished high school. As such, he often had difficulty finding work. At times, he would have to leave home to seek employment. At one point, Dad left for northern Labrador, where he built houses in an isolated Innu community as part of a government-sponsored project. At night, my mom and I would listen intently to the radio as we charted Dad's course with the comings and goings of the Labrador coastal boats.

At one point, Dad decided to pursue an automotive mechanic course at the local trades college. My dad had a practical intelligence that I could only dream of. He knew how to build a house and could fix a car or any type of machine. Home repairs are my nightmare. However, when it came to math, I could help.

One memory I hold dear is helping Dad with his math – fractions in particular. I felt so proud helping my dad with his math homework. For some reason, I still remember Dad tentatively working on the division of fractions, his pronounced script on the paper, with my explanations on how to divide them.

My proudest day was when Dad graduated with his auto mechanic papers. He eventually got good work as a heavy-duty mechanic. His final years of employment were spent as the caretaker of our local parish.

Work is key to our identity, to our sense of self-worth. Work is at the heart of human dignity. St. John Paul II's first encyclical, *Laborem Exercens* (1981), reflected on the notion of human work. God is revealed as the Creator God, labouring and calling all into existence. Work, whether manual or intellectual, determines what it means to be human.

I don't know what it means to be without work. I have never experienced the pain of months or years without a job. I cannot imagine such hardship, particularly in a world based on a wage economy.

My dad, soon to turn 85, can lay no claim to having had a career. No framed degrees ever adorned the walls of his home. He is the beneficiary of no fat pension.

Despite all that, or maybe because of it, Dad has a deep appreciation of life. He has simple tastes. He collects nothing. Fishing on the river is his special joy. An even greater satisfaction, I think, comes from his ability to use his deep practical skills and wisdom for his family. When my sister was awarded a Habitat for Humanity house, Dad was on the site daily, labouring for his only daughter.

That's the kind of work Dad was known for – the kind that gives generously, quietly, expecting nothing in return. Maybe that was the lesson I learned those many evenings at the kitchen table with my dad. As he struggled with his fractions, I was learning the true meaning of work – to give and not to count the cost.

Seeing the Back of God

It's not easy being Catholic these days. Maybe it never was.

Everywhere we turn, the tensions seem many – condoms and contraception, pro-choice and pro-life, woman priests and married priests, liberal and conservative, pedophilia, sexual abuse and child pornography, homosexuality and gay marriage, divorce, remarriage, and reception of the sacraments, stem cell research and human genetic engineering … Have I left anything out?

I admit to not knowing how we as a Church should move ahead on many of these issues. I wrestle with them, with the many arguments pro and con. I wrestle with my conscience, with the official teaching of the Church. I try to understand.

But in the end, I have come to see that the Church, and that means you and me, is both sinner and saint. We don't have it all together. We stumble, we shine, we falter and we proclaim.

We are called to speak of divine things, but human words can only do so much.

The priest is not God – instead, he tries to point, often in weak and feeble ways, to the coming Kingdom of God.

The Catholic Church is not God – instead, it tries to point, often in weak and feeble ways, to the coming Kingdom of God.

We are not God – instead, we try to point, often in weak and feeble ways, to the coming Kingdom of God.

Maybe we are called to speak more humbly of divine things, to proclaim with gusto the love and mercy of God. But when it comes to the tensions of our day, maybe we need to be more circumspect.

We can never see the face of God and live. We only see the back of God. If we accept this, then maybe we should be more willing to listen to those who speak differently than we do. That way, maybe they will be more patient with our own faltering steps as Church.

Truth and the Mystery of God

For some reason, I feel less and less attracted to truth.

That may sound strange from someone who is a member of a body of believers who profess that they have found the truth. It may even sound anti-intellectual or inconsistent from one who professes a deep desire for truth. Even worse, such a statement may come across as somewhat scandalous given my love of Jesus Christ, who is the Way, the Truth and the Life.

So, I must state right up front that I do not deny that Jesus Christ is indeed the Truth of the World, that the search for truth is a fundamental human vocation, and that truth does indeed exist.

That being said, I still am weary of much Christian talk about "truth." Why do I seem to have this allergic reaction to "truth"?

Increasingly, particularly in Church or faith circles, I hear a rallying cry for the profession of truth, for followers of Christ to be uncompromising in their explication and proclamation of the Christian truth.

Furthermore, this call for "truth" is often only expressed in moralistic terms. Tell us what the Church says we can and cannot do. Give us only solid doctrine.

What we often don't hear is an invitation to grow in intimacy with Jesus Christ, to develop a prayerful, discerning heart that seeks to live in the glory of the Paschal Mystery, to embrace a faith that gives life and life to the full. Increasingly, voices seem to clamour for boundaries, for walls, for clarification on who's "in" and who's "out."

I am not denying the need for "right order" or for proper ways of proceeding that build up the body of Christ. Good structure gives freedom and hope.

What I worry about is a Christian reflex that defines the world predominantly in terms of "us" and "them," of the initiated versus the uninitiated.

I worry about a Church that focuses on the Eucharist as a symbol of division, rather than a possible sign of unity, that equates too tightly *orthopraxis,* or right action, with *orthodoxy,* or right thought.

How different would our Church be if we focused on the mystery of God rather than the truth of God? How different would our vision of God be if we bowed our heads and hearts before the mystery of the divine rather than the truth of propositions?

I sense that God is not a problem to be solved, but rather a mystery into which we enter. The Mystery of God *is* the Truth of God. Jesus flipped the world around using strange, mysterious images. Die and you shall live. Give and you shall receive. The last shall be first and the first shall be last. He used mysterious parables that spoke of the mystery of the Kingdom of God.

Return to the River

My dad uses a cane on the river these days. Since he's 84 years old, I suppose that's allowed. It's an old bamboo ski pole, long past its prime, but works quite well as it steadies him through the rushing waters.

I write on the banks of the Colinet River in Newfoundland. It's a small river, barely reaching 30 to 50 metres wide through most of its 50-kilometre journey. Head-watered in Ripple Pond, it weaves through verdant forests of balsam fir, spruce and larch, slipping into the briny embrace of St. Mary's Bay.

The Colinet is home to a good run of Atlantic salmon that find their way back from their winter home in the icy waters off southern Greenland. Each year they return, strong and intent on their journey to their summer home in the backwaters of Newfoundland's Avalon Peninsula.

As the salmon return, so does my dad. He was weaned on fishing – or trouting, as we say in Newfoundland. He grew up not far from the waters of the Colinet River, on a homestead deeded by the government of Newfoundland to those men who served in the war effort. My grandfather served in the Scottish forests as a member of the Newfoundland Forestry Corps.

My dad is not an educated man in the contemporary sense of the term. No high school diploma is stuffed away in the family Bible. No university degree hangs from a wall. He can lay claim to none of these. But, as everyone knows, we cannot confuse education with intelligence.

My dad is an expert fly fisherman. Self-taught, or simply from years of practice, he can drop a fly on a dime – a dime of water, that is. He knows the pools and the eddies where the sea trout and salmon like to lie, resting on their instinctual journey. He knows when to fish, where to fish, how to fish.

I would not err too much in admitting that fishing on the river is sacred to my dad. Sacred in the sense of that which is most important; sacred in the sense of being ineffable. He has not spoken of it, but it is obvious; he is at home on the river. It's in his blood. Maybe things like that are never named by those like my dad. They are simply lived.

The largest trout my dad ever caught was a sea-run brown trout – all 20 pounds of fighting flesh, fresh from the sea. He caught it on Good Friday. No better day to catch fish. Fish, as well as fishing and fishermen, figure abundantly in Scripture.

I think that fishing and the river have become the pearl of great price for my dad. He knows what is of value – and he faithfully returns to the source of that energy. Maybe it's the quiet and the solitude. Maybe it's the dance of sun on rippled water, the silence of still waters running deep.

Or maybe it's a need – a visceral need that cannot be denied. A need to be with oneself amid the beauty of God. The constant flow of the waters, year in, year out, must have some effect on a man. Fishing all day on the river demands, or possibly engenders, a tranquility of heart. Otherwise, I reckon one would go crazy with the sound of one's thoughts.

When we had returned home, Dad reached into his sack and took out three fresh sprigs of the wild iris that grows on the banks of the Colinet River. My mother joyfully pruned them and settled the emerging violet in a pretty vase. After six decades of marriage, one could wish for no more.

Whatever it is for my father, no one will come to know. What my dad has learned from years on the river, he has not named. Maybe he can't. Maybe that's the way it should be.

Yes. I suspect that my dad cannot speak of why he, like the salmon, returns year after year to the same pool, to that same bend in the river. It's just something one must do. Or better still, it's just something one does.

In the end, the salmon and my dad are probably one and the same. Each year they return home. Each season they simply must return to the river, the river of life. This is as it should be, no matter what.

JULY

Of Forests, the Mind and the Soul

My years of Jesuit formation introduced me to a vast intellectual world beyond that of my scientific upbringing. Philosophy situated science within the broader intellectual tradition and invited me to grapple with the fundamental questions posed by humankind throughout the ages. Theology expanded my vision to a point from which it could never return. It allowed me to reflect on the question "Does matter really matter in the Christian tradition?" and provided me with the language to articulate my lifelong experience of nature as a theophany or visible manifestation of God.

The gift of doctoral studies in forest ecology plunged my mind and soul deep into the heart of matter, into the heart of creation. It was there that I found something more of Christ.

My research necessarily posed a well-defined scientific thesis. At the same time, I carried out the scientific research within a broader human context that permitted other questions: What meaning does nature have for human salvation? Does nature have a final destiny in and through God? What responsibility do we have towards the environment? What factors link the destruction of nature and the destitution of people?

I could pass my days in the solitude and beauty of the forest without being affected by the clamour and ugliness of the plundering of our forests, our seas, our lands and our human spirit. Come with me into the wilderness, says the Lord, and there I will speak tenderly to you (Hosea 2:14). And it is there that God spoke to me, seduced me, graced me and rooted me in the mystery of beauty and life.

I have been blessed by years of study. Such studies have been salvific, enabling a vision that began long ago during my childhood meanderings in the woods of Newfoundland. I was given the time and means to study my passion, to pull myself away in relative isolation to focus on the ways of my heart. I have always been grateful for such a gift.

The Society of Jesus, animated by the holiness of its founder, St. Ignatius of Loyola, strives to find God in all things. Jesuits, in company with many others, are growing in their awareness of the need to bear witness to the risen Christ at the heart of all creation, to the risen Christ in whom all things were made.

The 12th-century monk St. Bernard of Clairvaux (1090–1153) provides a sense of direction when, in a letter to a fellow Cistercian, he wrote: "Believe me, trees and stones will teach you that which you cannot learn from any master" (*Epistle* 106). I couldn't agree more. And so, I sit and listen to the voice of the forest.

Salvation in Forests – and Lichens

I was seduced at an early age – tempted by rock, wind and water, invited by peatland, heath and forest, infatuated by nature and wildness. Enthralled, obsessed, blinded, I fell for nature. My affair continues.

On the far eastern edge of North America, near the confluence of the cold Labrador Current and the warm Gulf Stream, the rhythm of the North Atlantic moulded me. The ebb and flow of tide and wave, dense fog banks, migrating whales, screeching gulls and briny, mesmerizing winds nurtured me.

It was to the interior forests of my homeland that I was drawn – to that often fog-strewn mosaic of forest, bog and heath that stretched to the horizon and beyond. Many days did I spend tramping those sylvan wilds with family and friends, trout fishing, berry picking – or as was often the case, simply spending time in solitude. My nursemaid, my companion, my God, these forests spoke of mystery, of love, of divine silence.

It's hard to explain, but the forest helps me to find my voice. The forest does not judge or suggest, but simply opens space and time to contemplation. The winds are muffled, the rain absorbed, the snowfall softened. To enter the forest is to enter the depth of stillness, the heart of solitude.

The forest interior stills my heart and soul, attunes my senses, permitting me to see and hear in new ways. I am at home. My muscles relax, my pace slows, and my heart softens. Maybe that's why the monastic monks of old and new fled to the forests in search of sublime solitude. To mountaintops, to watered valleys or to secluded forests do monks of old and of our time go to cleanse their souls and hearts.

When I enter the forest, an immediate sense of wonder and curiosity overwhelms me. My eye ferrets out the myriad of form and shape, the hue and tone of colour, the shifting waves of light and motion. The primordial beauty, the very "given-ness" of life and form and motion intrigues me. And so, I enter the forest with a deep sense of expectation, of anticipation before things unknown.

For the past several years, lichens of the forests, indeed lichens in all places, have captured my imagination. What is it that intrigues me? Is it the excitement of the chase, of lichen hunting? Or the expectation that I will discover a new record, or even a new species? Or maybe the desire to name, to order, to relate all that I see around me? All this, to be sure, and much more.

What the poet William Blake (1757–1827) wrote in his 1803 poem "Auguries of Innocence" resonates deeply:

> To see a world in a grain of sand,
> And a heaven in a wild flower,
> Hold infinity in the palm of your hand,
> And eternity in an hour.

I presume that this lichen attraction is of God. I hope that it's no novel neurosis or fetish. This lichen love is so non-utilitarian, so "useless" that it can only be of God, I think – at least for me. My mind plays with lichens and delights in them.

Other than that, I wish I could tell you what happens to me. But I can't, really. Maybe that's what love does. Maybe that's who God is. Unnameable, mysterious, delightful.

What Good Are Lichens?

I knew I had not seen it before. Full of anticipation, I examined it under my 10x hand lens. Sure enough, it was new to my eyes. I called my colleague over to have a look and he confirmed my suspicions – we had found something new for Newfoundland. A month or so later, I showed my find to another colleague, a professional lichenologist and director of the herbarium at the New Brunswick Museum. No question about it, we had found a lichen new not only to Newfoundland, but new to North America! Better yet, the macrolichen was considered endemic to southern Norway. In other words, I had discovered the first incidence of this lichen outside of southern Norway.

Before I continue, dear reader, I should stop here and note something that's probably on your mind. You may wonder if I have lichen on *my* mind. Actually, I do. Every day, I work away at the draft of the Annotated Catalogue of the Lichens and Lichenicolous Fungi of Newfoundland and Labrador. My holidays are devoted to lichen hunting in the field. They've become something of a passion, a naturalist's delight, a wonder to behold. I digress, so let's continue with the story.

First described in 1982, *Parmeliopsis esorediata* (Degel.) Nordnes had been known from only 22 locations in southern Norway. The discovery in Newfoundland poses a series of interesting questions, particularly with respect to its global distribution. Some lichens exhibit what is called an amphi-Atlantic distribution: they are found on both sides of the north Atlantic, along the seaboards of eastern North America and western Europe. The Atlantic Ocean began to form during the Jurassic period, about 150 million years ago, when a rift developed in the supercontinent of Gondwanaland, resulting in the separation of the Americas from Europe and Africa. The separation continues today at the rate of several centimetres a year along the Mid-Atlantic Ridge. The Norway and Newfoundland populations of *Parmeliopsis esorediata* are growing farther apart.

St. Thomas Aquinas (1225–1274) wrote that God created the diversity of organisms to communicate the divine goodness. Any one creature could not adequately express the fullness of the divine goodness. Only a diversity of creatures was adequate to the job. St. Bonaventure saw all of creation as a revelation or self-expression of the blessed Trinity.

People often ask, "What good are lichens?" Lichens possess many ecological functions, not the least of which is their essential and indispensable role in the nutrition of the vast caribou herds of the northern hemisphere.

But despite this and other ecological roles played by lichens, I like to respond that lichens are good simply because God said so. Simply by existing, lichens, as do all creatures, give glory to God. That's a good enough reason for me.

Almost every Sunday we pray *Gloria in excelsis Deo* – Glory to God in the highest! Lichens do the same, albeit in a slightly different fashion.

The Naming of Things

I didn't know what it was. But I did know it was a new species. A new species! I felt giddy with excitement. A species of lichen never described or named by anyone. Maybe never even seen by anyone before. My colleague suggested that I contact a California lichenologist who was a specialist in this group of lichens. If anyone would know how best to proceed, it would be him.

Eventually, I sent the unknown species to the specialist and was able to meet him in my travels. Sure enough, the species was undescribed and was new to science. But, there was a glitch. More work was needed on a related lichen genus before my find could be placed into its proper genus.

Eventually, the newly described species saw the light of day with the name *Acarospora maccarthyi* K. Knudsen and Kourouck.

The lichen genus *Acarospora* currently holds about 200 species of lichenized fungi, all of which grow on rock. The genus name is Greek for tiny spores; *acaro* (*akares*, meaning tiny; and *spora*, meaning spore). Kerry Knudsen and Jana Kocourková, a husband-and-wife team at the Czech University of Life Sciences Prague, in the Czech Republic, described and named the species. Those who describe a new species have the right to name it as they wish.

You may note that the epithet *maccarthyi* is named for me, but rendered slightly differently from my name. There's a reason for this. The naming of species must follow strict rules developed and cared for by taxonomic specialists who have produced the International Code of Nomenclature for algae, fungi and plants. According to section 60C.5a of the Code, "the Scottish patronymic prefix 'Mac', 'Mc', or 'M', meaning 'son of', should be spelled 'mac' and united with the rest of the name." I worried about the loss of my familiar surname, but after a good night's sleep, I promptly forgot about it and moved on.

In the book of Genesis, God creates the beasts of the field and the birds of the sky, then brings them to the man, Adam, to see what he would call them. Whatever Adam called a living creature, that was its name (Genesis 2:20).

Naming all the species on the planet is a tricky affair. A 2011 study estimated that there are approximately 8.7 million eukaryotic organisms (organisms made up of cells containing membrane-bound organelles, such as a nucleus) on Earth; 86% of existing species on Earth and 91% of existing species in the oceans still await description. That's a lot of new future names. This study only examined eukaryotic organisms. As for prokaryotic organisms (those not made up of cells containing membrane-bound organelles), such as bacteria, a 2016 study estimated that 99.999% of the globe's estimated 1 trillion microbial species remain undiscovered.

All this to say that we have a long way to go before we can hope to name even a tiny fraction of our planet's biodiversity. With current extinction rates being 100 to 1,000 times greater than the natural background extinction rate, the implications are obvious. We will lose many species to extinction before we even know they existed.

To give a name: what a wonderful gift. Parents with their newborn children, and lichenologists with their newfound lichens. A name permits a relationship. No longer is the other unknown, but is now named and given a place of honour. A mutuality is assured. The Creator Trinity is seen in a whole different light. Such creative, marvellous fecundity in a God who is the maker of all things visible and invisible.

With another lichenologist, this time from Frankfurt, Germany, I have named another new lichen from Newfoundland. This one we named *Biatora terrae-novae* Printzen & McCarthy, after the province of Newfoundland, where it was first discovered. One of the latest members of the *Biatora* genus, this species normally grows on mossy trees and is, to date, known only from Newfoundland.

The naming of two new lichen species. A seeming drop in the bucket when you consider the millions of taxa yet to be named. But one cannot let the magnitude of such a challenge chill the will or stymie one's action. To name a new creature is a God-given mandate. It's worthy of all our effort and skill and finesse.

Sylvan Retreat

I have always been drawn off the beaten path into the forest. The open places have I eschewed. I have always longed for the edge places, ferreting out the nooks and crannies, remnant woods and groves, aching for wildness, for things primeval. Around the next corner, over the next hill, across the next hollow. I have lingered around the field, along streams, through open gardens, but for some reason, it is the woods that continue to call me. I'm still looking for what I have yet to find.

I find that easing from field into forest is not always easy. A transition must be breached. The seemingly clear and crisp boundaries are in fact blurred. The way is usually entangled with chaotic growth. No path exists.

One such transition took me to a place I have revisited many a time. At the foot of the field below the old hermitage, at the back of the property, away from the highway, the path skirts a forest that seemed to beckon me one day. I left the brilliance of the dry alfalfa field that rippled with wind, amid the cacophony of crickets and grasshoppers. An entanglement of vines, waist-high goldenrod, ubiquitous glossy and black buckthorn, and sturdy burdock impeded my progress. My effort and persistence eventually paid off. A few metres beyond the edge, into the coolness, I was welcomed by leafy stillness and fluorescence.

Sound gave way to silence, heat to cool. The dry grains and grasses of human design gave way to the wild and cool offerings of the forest floor. Jack-in-the-pulpit, enchanter's nightshade, wild ginger, false Solomon's seal, and the delicate racemes of snow-flowered foamflower and the two-leaved bishop's cap replaced the hardy weeds and growings of human intention. Decayed nurse logs were covered with rows of wild sarsaparilla. The succulent, translucent spotted jewelweed thickened the dried-up swamp in the late of summer.

Axe and plough, field and furrow, the sweat and blood of labour have not entered here. I had passed from human fabrication to Divine creation, from human intention to contemplation. The imposed pattern of our agriculture was replaced by the pattern and process of the forest.

Reflections on such floristic transitions could not help but instil a lament, a gnawing, persistent sense of loss. Lament at the loss of the rich biodiversity of the moist deciduous forests before the wave of field grass and clover. The forest plants are all native. The field plants are all exotic, brought into this land by intention or folly.

How to describe such a sense of loss? The absent myriad flashes of colour and form, odour and texture of the forest.

Replaced by the banal, the predictable and the common of the field. The simplification of both nature and culture. The domestication of the wild. The end of the wild. The Latin term *vulgaris* (common) describes many of these introduced weeds. Following humans around the globe, they have replaced the rare and gorgeous with the ordinary; vulgar, indeed.

In many ways, this forest grove simply is. And therein lies its beauty and meaning. Into its arms you enter. Before its gaze you stand in awe. Within its silence you rest. While on retreat, this secluded grove of majestic red and silver maple became my chapel, my cathedral. Each day, it drew me beyond the retreat house, down the well-trod path, away from the field, into myself, into something of God. And there I sat, propped against a hardened red maple trunk, knees bent, feet firmly planted on a moss-covered log lying upon the rich leaf-layered forest floor.

My hidden forest nook became for me a sacred grove: sacred as it spoke to me of life and spirit that fed my soul. My guard lessened. My heart awakened. I was able to wait, to listen, to rest, to take root in the moment, embraced by the solitude of the forest. A complexity of green, ordered to life and continuity, the forest enacted no toll, no price. For me, it spoke something of the Divine. Was not this created grove a mirror, an image of its Creator? In the midst of the forest, something, someone, spoke to me in ways ineffable. Come with me into the forest. And there I will speak to your heart.

AUGUST

Jesuits and Heavenly Bodies

I have always enjoyed looking at heavenly bodies … heavenly bodies in space, that is.

I remember well those early years gazing into the dark night skies of Newfoundland, far from any town or city. I was mesmerized by that bright band of stars straddling the heavens, the so-called Milky Way that contains up to 400 billion stars across more than 100,000 light years of blackened space.

Some Jesuits get to be stargazers all their lives. A few years ago, in Vancouver, I met Fr. José Funes, S.J., the former director of the Vatican Observatory. An Argentinean by birth, Fr. José studies the kinematics and dynamics of disk galaxies, star formation in the Milky Way, and the relationship between gravitational interaction and galactic activity. The current director of the Observatory, an American Jesuit, Br. Guy Consolmagno, S.J., is a planetary geologist who studies asteroids and meteorites. This "Pope's Astronomer" even has a minor planet or asteroid named in his honour. 4597 Consolmagno, named in 1983, takes 4.21 years to orbit the sun. A nice way to give glory to the beauty of God's creation. A nice way to be priest – and religious brother.

It's not only I who thinks that. So does the Pope and the Holy See. Since the 1930s, the Vatican has entrusted the operation of the Vatican Observatory to the Society of Jesus.

The Vatican Observatory was founded in 1891 by Pope Leo XIII (1810–1903). Before that, however, the Church, and particularly the Jesuits, were actively involved in astronomical research since Pope Gregory XIII (1502–1585) employed the help of Jesuits and others in the reform of the Roman calendar in 1582.

Headquartered at Castel Gandolfo, the papal summer residence, the Vatican Observatory operates the Vatican Advanced Technology Telescope (VATT) at the Mount Graham International Observatory in Arizona. Jesuits with the talent and desire are missioned to doctoral studies in astronomy for work at the Observatory.

Fr. David Brown, S.J., an American, recently completed his PhD in astronomy at Oxford University; he has been assigned to the Observatory as a researcher on the evolution of stars. Congolese Jesuit Fr. Jean-Baptiste Kikwaya, S.J., studies meteors, fireballs and near-Earth objects. Fr. Richard D'Souza, S.J., of India spends his time trying to figure out the formation and evolution of galaxies.

I'm a bit envious of these brother Jesuits. They get to tinker with telescopes. They visit observatories on the tops of exotic mountains above the clouds. They are paid to gaze at the stars. But most of all, they get to proclaim by their lives that "the heavens are telling the glory of God" (Psalm 19:1). But, I suppose that's our vocation as well. We just have to do it in different ways.

Reverence for the Heavens

The Astrophysical Journal, published by the 118-year-old American Astronomical Society, is considered the world's foremost research journal devoted to all aspects of astronomy and astrophysics.

Two recent articles in *The Astrophysical Journal* have set me thinking.

The first research paper, published in 2013, is entitled "Weighing 'El Gordo' with a Precision Scale: Hubble Space Telescope Weak-lensing Analysis of the Merging Galaxy Cluster ACT-CL J0102-4915 at z=0.87."

I never imagined that a telescope, even an orbiting telescope, could weigh a galaxy. But that is exactly what this astronomical team did. They determined the mass of the largest cluster of galaxies known from the early universe – and named it, appropriately, *El Gordo* (the fat one). Located more than 7 billion light years from Earth (when the universe was half its current age), the galaxy boasts a mass 3 quadrillion times that of the sun. Three quadrillion – that's 3 followed by 15 zeros.

Apparently, this discovery will help us better understand the concept of dark matter and dark energy in the universe. The regular matter that makes up what we normally consider as being composed of matter, such as humans, stars and coffee cups, constitutes only 5% of the universe. The rest of the stuff is a complete mystery. It seems that 27% of the known universe is dark matter. Up to 6% of the universe we call dark energy.

In other words, a whopping 95% of all the mass and energy in the universe is still a mystery to us. What we see and experience daily is only a fraction of what our universe is. And this includes all that our best instruments can detect and measure.

The second article, published in the 2016 issue of *The Astrophysical Journal*, announced the detection of the farthest known galaxy in the universe – a remarkably luminous galaxy at $Z = 11.1$ measured with Hubble Space Telescope grism spectroscopy.

The Hubble Space Telescope imaged a tiny but bright galaxy located at 13.4 billion light years from Earth. That means that the infant galaxy was forming only 400 million years after the Big Bang, when the universe began. In these images, we peer back into the early reaches of the universe. The galactic light, travelling at 300,000 km per second, has taken 13.4 billion years to reach us.

I don't know about you, but such numbers boggle my mind. Our scientific discoveries, particularly of the heavens, never fail to amaze and entrance me.

I am drawn to wonder, invited into mystery teased open by the insights of science. There's a sacred depth to creation, to nature, to the worlds that our minds are privileged to meet.

Unfortunately, such scientific insights often provoke different reactions in people. For some, the power of our mathematical insight into nature necessarily excludes any notion of the divine or the transcendent. Faith in God is construed as the enemy of scientific progress and human well-being. An evolutionary science, for example, resting on its great explanatory power, pushes evolution beyond its bounds and presents it as a "first philosophy" with the ability to fully and completely describe what it means to be human.

On the flip side are those frightened by what they perceive as a "Godless" or "soulless" science. So-called creationists, for example, conflate science and religion to the point where the Bible is understood as a book of science, giving us all the God-ascribed answers to our cosmological or scientific questions. Science is feared, and the image of God is narrowed to a point not recognized in Scripture.

In his 1988 letter to the Vatican Observatory, St. John Paul II called for a deep and ongoing dialogue between science and theology. According to the former Pope, this dialogue was crucial. He noted that "science can purify religion from error and superstition" while "religion can purify science from idolatry and false absolutes."

We live in only one world – a world that is described by both science and faith. Each needs the other to help us to be fully human.

The Priest as Expert Dispensing Truth to Others

Priests are often cast in the role of experts dispensing truth to others. Such an understanding is often accorded to other professionals, including doctors, lawyers and scientists.

I am quite uncomfortable with such an understanding of priest.

This discomfort does not mean that I fail to see the priest as having anything to say. Far from it. If such were the case, I'd have to close up shop and speak no more. However, it's the kind of truth that I question.

There used to be a time when people believed all that Father said. From the bedroom to the boardroom, no topic or issue lay beyond the bounds of priestly exhortation. How times have changed. Nowadays, the credibility of priests is often hard won.

The problem lies, I think, with our understanding of truth. By this I mean a sort of conceptual truth where we assume to capture the mystery of God in clear, well-defined, distinct ideas and propositions. When this model of truth dominates our conversations, then our only response is univocal – the answer must be either true or false. And then the battle of supremacy begins, as one side fights against the other in the war for truth. The victorious and the vanquished are the only result.

However, there is more to Jesus Christ than simply truth. He is the Way, the Truth and the Life. What's real is much richer than simply true propositional statements. For Christians, truth is not simply a statement of fact, of the so-called truths of the faith. For Christians, truth is a person, the God-Man Jesus Christ.

I like the thought of St. Paul in his letter to the Church in Ephesus when he invites his listeners to experience the "breadth and length and height and depth" of the love of Christ and "to know the love of Christ that surpasses knowledge, so that you may be filled with all the fullness of God" (Ephesians 3:18-19).

The priest cannot help but speak the truth of God, but that truth is not simply a series of conceptual statements. For who in their right mind would ever claim to know the "mind of God"? The truth we seek or the truth we profess is not a set of clear and distinct ideas, but rather stumblings into the Mystery of God.

I believe the truth of God is approached only on bended knee, with shoes removed and heads bowed low. We can never see the face of God and live. God is best viewed tangentially, not in the sound and fury of thunder and lightning, but rather in the gentle whispers found deep within our heart.

We do not speak the truth of God; rather, we witness the truth of God. At times, words are good and necessary, and the clearer and simpler are those words, the better. But such words must be rooted in the crucible of life, in the heartbreak of life and prayer.

As Fr. Richard Rohr, O.F.M., is fond of saying, human experience has taught us that the best way to know God is through great suffering or great love. Often love and suffering are one and the same thing. From there flow the energy and power to speak the word of truth.

The greatest Word spoken by God was the cross of Christ. From such suffering love did the truth of God explode into creation. We should expect nothing else. Only from the cross can the priest (and indeed all followers of Christ) speak the truth of life.

Greetings in Vancouver

I knew I was back home in Vancouver when I saw both of them on the same day.

From a distance, I knew who it was. The characteristic limp identified him from afar. He was dressed in an overcoat, his sack on his back, umbrella slung down along his side, tuque on his head. It must have been 25 degrees Celsius. But that didn't seem to matter.

I had often attempted eye contact, uttered a greeting as we passed each other along the street or along Jericho Beach. Each time, I hoped for a response. Once, I thought he looked my way, or maybe it was simply my imagination, rooted in a desire for contact.

Why I have this desire, I know not. Maybe it's because of the regularity of our contact. I have walked Jericho Beach for several years now, and no one else has crossed my path like he has. It's like clockwork at times. As if we start out at the same time, take opposite directions towards each other – only to pass with a furtive acknowledgement.

The other person meets me in a different way. We have never walked past each other in the street. It is I who always walk past her. The coffee shop window separates our gaze upon each other. There she sits, in the same seat, facing the same direction, in the same coffee shop, on the same street. Her coffee or tea in one hand, a half-eaten sandwich listless on her plate, her gaze paling into the distance. Along I walk, briskly, intent on the day, but I too always walk in the same direction, up the same street, towards the same destination.

I return to Vancouver after several months of travel in eastern Canada. Weeks of meetings, fieldwork, adventure, retreat, family, friends … Torngat Mountains National Park. Emails to answer, books to read, films to watch, lichens to collect. People calling me, enjoying my company, and I theirs. Life, abundant life, with hope and expectancy.

What of this young man and this old woman? How has the summer treated them? Who has called upon them? Who has asked for their opinion? Who has inquired about their hopes and dreams?

Their days have probably remained much the same over the past three months. Maybe I am rather presumptuous and know not of what I speak. But I hazard to guess that not much has changed since last we passed each other on the street.

I have always wanted to slow down when I approach the man, to greet him boldly and to ask him about his day. But for some reason, probably many reasons, my voice remains mute. I take the easy road and simply pass by with a smile and a quiet hello.

Maybe I fear that any energetic greeting would be met with bewilderment or rejection – or, heaven forbid, acceptance. What would I do then? I would have to stop, not think of the next task that awaits me at the end of my walk, disrupt my schedule for that day. Beware of what you desire – you may just get it.

And so, we continue to meet in passing. I like to think that they recognize me by now. They notice my gait, my routine.

Furthermore, I hope they think kindly of me, as I do of them. We may never actually meet, shake hands or greet each other with more than a one-way word. Maybe some meetings are meant to be that way – a meeting of the heart, I like to think. I hope I am right.

A Morning with the Pope

In my neck of the woods, we don't see many Popes. Thus it was with a child-like excitement that I joined my brother Jesuits from across the globe on the morning of October 24, 2016, to await the arrival of Pope Francis and his address to the 36th General Congregation of the Society of Jesus. What would he say to us? Would he ask something special of us? Some of us may have been looking for a peg upon which to hang our apostolic hats. Others may have hoped for a papal-approved sense of direction.

Pope Francis gifted us with what we may have least expected, but what we probably needed the most. He brought us back to the Formula of our Institute, to the foundational inspiration of St. Ignatius and his companions. By doing this, he showed great respect for the Society of Jesus. A concrete apostolic focus would have been easy. But it would have been rather paternalistic, and in the end, a failure of hope for the Society of Jesus and the global Ignatian family.

Pope Francis, however, grounded us in *our way of proceeding* that expresses for us the best manner by which the greater good is accomplished. Concretely, Pope Francis characterized our way of proceeding that is marked by joy and consolation, the cross of Christ, and at the service of the Church, our Mother.

Human joy has been a central theme for Pope Francis – the joy of family, the joy of creation, the joy of the Gospel. He invited us to actively and incessantly seek the joy of consolation in decision making. Joy then becomes the criterion of action. In desolation, we wait, actively seeking the joy of consolation before we step forward in action. In consolation, we act with confidence and direction.

Our joy is mysteriously rooted in the cross of Christ. Touch my wounds, says Jesus to Thomas. Put your hand into my wounds and you will believe. Only by touching the wounds of Christ would Thomas make his great profession of faith: "My Lord and my God!" (John 20:28). No less is asked of us. We are to gaze into our own wounds and see how God has been so merciful to us. Only then will we be able to listen with compassion to the cry of the poor and the cry of the earth, the broken and crucified body of Christ.

We do all this as the body of Christ, as a community, as the Church. Discerning what to do in a Church that is both sinner and saint, free and broken, is our call as servants of God's Church. This demands of us the greatest spiritual freedom, a freedom that listens and offers hope.

I am very grateful for Pope Francis' challenge to the Society of Jesus. No obvious concrete mission fell from the lips of the Holy Father. We were given no specific task for which an apostolic plan could be developed in the years to come. It is obvious, however, that we were indeed given a mission, and a rather difficult one at that.

SEPTEMBER

Meetings in the Spirit

Meetings are not always easy. As Captain Kirk of the USS *Enterprise* is reported to have said, "Meetings are events where minutes are taken and hours wasted." Whether this aphorism can be legitimately attributed to Captain Kirk is beside the point; we can all relate.

As Jesuits, whenever we and our colleagues meet, we generally try to use a technique that we call "spiritual conversation." It's a way to meet that is not common in the corporate boardroom – nor in the parish council, for that matter.

What is spiritual conversation? It is not necessarily about spiritual things. Spiritual conversation is defined not by the subject matter of discussion, but rather by the quality of listening and the quality of speaking.

Spiritual conversation assumes "speaking from the heart," sharing "felt knowledge" or what is truly from our reflective experience. It does not concern what others may think, nor is it rooted in power or self-seeking. It simply shares one's inner awareness based on active listening to the stirrings of one's heart.

Spiritual conversation assumes trust in one's own experience and that of another. It grounds a stance of active listening and speaking. Lack of trust in the other, in oneself or in the process will shut down conversation and turn a meeting into a bloody affair where "minutes are taken and hours wasted." Trust, however, opens a conversation, instils freedom, and enables each person to speak and listen freely.

Free and trusted active listening and speaking may be engendered by using some simple tools. Five basic tools are available; check-in, first round of personal sharing, second round of reflective sharing, third round of discussion, and finally, a review of the meeting.

In the check-in, each person is invited to share, in a word or two, how they are feeling as they come to the meeting. We all bring different feelings to each meeting: fear, happiness, tiredness, preoccupation, etc. Articulation of these interior feelings sets a good tone for the meeting.

In the first round, participants share their experience of prayer, a talk, a document, etc. Each person is invited to speak one after the other. This is not a time for discussion or argumentation, but rather active listening to what others have to say. People share their feelings, their experience, their thoughts.

In the second round, participants are invited to share how they have been affected by what they heard in the first round. This important round attempts to discern and identify shared communal movements within the group, dissonant movements, and so on. Second-round sharing is often shorter than first-round sharing, and people are invited to speak when they're ready, in no particular order.

In the third round, participants engage in an open discussion that may include agreement and disagreement, with the normal give and take typical of discussions. The first two rounds of sharing should give this round of discussion a quality of conversation that is free from the divisive manifestation of self-centredness and ego flexing.

Finally, the review is a short, reflective act of awareness that looks back over the whole meeting.

I have witnessed the efficacy of such spiritual conversation in countless meetings. Each person, regardless of "position," is heard. The depth of sharing would not have been possible otherwise. I witnessed the power of the Spirit at work in the group.

Working together demands meetings. The simple tools of spiritual conversation can greatly aid such meetings. Spiritual conversation invites active listening, putting the best interpretation on what others say, and an active and deep awareness of what we think and feel. Trust and freedom are engendered. Meetings then become events where minutes are taken and hours are *not* wasted.

Do You See What I See?
Interreligious Dialogue

St. Ignatius, founder of the Jesuits, is reported to have said that saving words move both the mind and the heart. That's exactly what happened, I think, as I once listened to Rabbi Dr. Robert Daum at an evening talk given for Catholic Campus Ministry at the University of British Columbia. I was personally moved by his strength of mind and his open heart. At one point in his talk, I found tears welling up in my eyes in response to his desire for truth and his obvious acceptance of the complexities of the human heart before the vagaries of personal, religious and political life.

Sibling relations are often the most difficult. Civil wars are often the most violent and reprehensible. So, too, the dialogue among the great monotheistic faiths of Judaism, Islam and Christianity can be the most difficult.

Rabbi Daum began by focusing on some general characteristics of authentic dialogue. Dialogue, he maintained, is possible only in an atmosphere of what he termed "epistemological doubt." In other words, authentic doubt is essential to conversation. Not a doubt marked by nihilism or relativism, but a humble acknowledgement of how much there is to learn from the other. We will always be marked by an existential distance, an incommensurability, an existential aloneness that marks a gap that can never be fully breached. Rather than precluding dialogue, such distances invite us to dialogue with respect and not a little trembling. The conversation assumes that we have entered into holy land that seeks not necessarily a common theology, but rather a common and familiar vocabulary.

Think of the three terms "Israel," "Palestine" and "the Holy Land." Three terms that cover the same geography, but vastly different conceptual spaces. In fact, these are contested spaces that defy a common meaning at present. I experienced the same in northern Labrador last summer. For me, I was travelling in a vast wilderness landscape. For my Inuk guide, however, it was a lived landscape, full of memory and meaning: over there he shot his first caribou as a boy. And there, that's where his mother took them berry picking in the fall. The same landscape – two very different "inscapes." Any true dialogue between me and my Inuk guide on the meaning of that same land would require a certain depth of soul and mind that is not possible in a 30-second sound bite.

Another moment that moved my heart and soul was Rabbi Daum's reflection on our use of what he termed "the language of shame." In any intense debate, we are often tempted, in our moral outrage, to employ weapons of shame against one another. Catholics and other people of God can so easily resort to the language of "conservative" or "liberal," or worse, as we attempt to shame others to accept our way of thinking. True prophets, however, are never self-proclaimed. Only history will make that judgment. True prophets are both teacher and learner. Let us sit down and learn together. Only then will there be hope for a future together.

Are we all now singing a common song of solidarity and communion? Not at all. Rabbi Daum underscored the inherently complex historical, conceptual, cultural and theological differences that divide us. Many communities of faith are conflicted – both from within and from outside.

My spiritual director, ever patient with my wayward peregrinations, is quick to remind me that "holiness is in the struggle." I like that. It seems that I have no other choice as I struggle to make sense of my life and its role in the bigger picture. Rabbi Daum, it seems, is called to be in the midst of that struggle for understanding. I like to think that he has chosen well. Each year on Holy Thursday evening we are invited to enter the mystery of dialogue and authentic conversation. It's not a tea party, to be sure, but then neither was the Last Supper.

What Christians May Learn from Atheists

I am reading a fascinating book by Tomáš Halík, a Czech Roman Catholic priest and winner of the 2014 Templeton Prize. The 2009 book is entitled *Patience with God: The Story of Zacchaeus Continuing in Us.*

Fr. Tomáš writes about atheism. He knows the impact of atheism first hand. He trained "underground" for the Catholic priesthood in his native Czechoslovakia during the years of oppressive Communist rule. For 11 years, even his mother was unaware that he had been ordained a priest.

According to Halík, the story of Zacchaeus (Luke 19:1-10) continues in us all. We're all a bit like Zacchaeus, curious about Jesus but not wanting to get too close.

At a distance, up a tree, we peer our way through the leafy branches, partly hidden, partly straining to see. Intrigued by Jesus, but not willing to join the crowd, we are content to observe Jesus from a distance.

Expressed more starkly, it may be said that we all harbour a bit of atheism. For some it's strong; for others, less so. For some, it blows hot and cold, or is stained by anger and cynicism. For most of us, however, it may simply be a healthy and wholesome doubt and questioning at the heart of faith.

At one time, we thought atheism was a sin. Anyone who professed atheism was deemed morally defective. In such cases, error had no rights, we thought. Or we assumed that sound and well-reasoned apologetics were all that were needed to steer unbelievers from their negligent ways.

With Zacchaeus as his guide, Halík takes a different approach to atheism. He asks, "What is the Spirit of God saying through contemporary atheism?"

You may ask, "How could the Spirit of God speak through disbelief in that very Spirit?" But Halík's question is not idle or frivolous.

Could God be speaking to the Church through the disbelief of our brothers and sisters? St. Ignatius of Loyola urges us to "see God in all things" – in all things, even in atheism.

The Second Vatican Council invites us to "read the signs of the times" (*Gaudium et Spes*, no. 4). Well, if there ever was a "sign of the times," it surely is atheism of one form or another. In the year 1500, most if not all Europeans would have been believers. Today, over 500 years later, the opposite is true.

Different and varied forces have no doubt contributed to this rise in atheism; the scientific revolution of the 16th century, the rise of the nation state, philosophical shifts that focused on the liberation and personal autonomy of the human person, to state just a few.

I wonder, however, if there is anything in our Catholic practice and way of thinking that has engendered and promoted disbelief in God. Maybe we forgot the call of God to truly love the world, the world in all its splendour and in all its need. Do people see the Church as suffering with the aches and pains of the world? Do people witness a humble Church intent on seeking and welcoming truth wherever it may be found?

I have no answers to these questions. But I wonder if we as Church are called to look up into the sycamore trees of the world and to invite those who look in at a distance, "Come down quickly, for I must stay at your house." Not our house, but their house, the house of disbelief. And so, Zacchaeus came down quickly and received Jesus with joy.

Leaving on a Jet Plane

When my Jesuit Provincial missioned me to Vancouver several years ago to work as chaplain at the University of British Columbia, I was not a happy camper. In fact, I thought that his decision was downright crazy. I was enjoying working on lichen research with the Newfoundland and Labrador Wildlife Division. Vancouver was not on my radar.

I was extremely dissatisfied with the Provincial's decision. Or maybe I was simply afraid. This is some of what I wrote to him: "I question the process by which you made this decision. I did not discern it in any proper manner, decisions seem to have been made rather quickly without any ongoing consultation with me, and the assignment deviates significantly from what I was originally assigned to do and to be." (The original assignment referred to my doctoral studies in forest ecology at the University of British Columbia.)

The Provincial responded by noting that my protests caused him to reconsider his decision – but only for a second.

So when I finally arrived in Vancouver, I was sure that the Provincial had made a mistake. How wrong I was.

I loved being on a university campus. It's a privileged place – a place of learning, a place of questioning. To be human is to question, to seek truth in love. It's a marvellous place where our faith and our reason can embrace in healthy tension.

The students taught me much. As I slip beyond middle age, whatever that means, I sense that I'm on the other side of life. Their vitality, intelligence and compassion kept me young and assured me that Jesus Christ will never abandon his Church.

The beauty of "supernatural BC" encouraged my soul and body. The North Shore mountains nursed my spirit. I marvelled, for the first time ever, at the beauty and brightness of alpine meadows flush with colourful flowers amid brilliant snowfields.

I learned that friendship must never be taken for granted. Friendship is a divine gift and can never be demanded or even assumed. It simply happens, like the passage of time. People weave themselves in and out of our lives to produce a rich and varied tapestry. Friendship demands time and energy, selfless giving and compassionate understanding.

Finally, I learned that God is forever faithful. The Bible shouts this hope-filled truth, a truth to which I am often deaf. Those years with the students in British Columbia revealed that God never abandons – and that his grace is indeed enough.

My next Provincial assigned me anew – this time to Toronto to work as his Socius, his companion and confidant in the care of the life and mission of the Jesuits in Canada.

So, in the words of John Denver (1943–1997), "kiss me and smile for me, hold me like you'll never let me go." I'm leaving on a jet plane – again. Think of me well – and smile if you can. Hold me in prayer, as I will you. And, may God continue to bless us – wherever life takes us.

I Miss My Guinness

The homecare nurse carefully and gently offered the spoonful of food to the priest's mouth. It was obvious that she was an old hand at feeding people. Another spoonful and the meal was finished. She softly wiped his mouth and lifted off his bib. The priest nodded and smiled.

At some point in our lives, we may come to a point where we can no longer feed ourselves. That time had finally arrived for my friend Fr. Brendan Boland, C.Ss.R.

Fr. Brendan, born in the Gaelic stronghold of western Ireland, had been a Redemptorist missionary in India and itinerant preacher throughout western Canada. I came to meet him during my days as chaplain at the University of British Columbia. He lived in the neighbouring Redemptorist parish, retired after his many years of apostolic life.

Advancing age was not to keep him down. Often, he would be seen waiting for the city bus, making his way out to the university or about town. In true Irish fashion, he loved the horse races. And, for some reason, he loved to join me for mass at St. Mark's Chapel, the home of the Catholic chaplaincy at UBC.

I don't remember how we hit it off, but we did. So much so that I looked forward to his company at mass on Sundays. Maybe it was the joyous humility that spilled out of him at every turn. Or maybe it was his generous encouragement of the work I was doing. He became something of a grandfather for me, I would say. He also became my regular confessor.

I remember well our times at a local pub where we would enjoy some fresh fish 'n' chips washed down by a full-bodied Guinness. He was a notable figure in some Vancouver pubs. The reason? He had translated their English menu into Irish Gaelic. English was his second language – he learned it as a young boy.

I enjoyed having him join me for the annual St. Patrick's mass when he would lead us in a Gaelic Our Father.

As I watched the homecare nurse feeding Fr. Brendan, I couldn't help but think about my own mortality. How would I live my final days? Not a morbid question, but simply a little realism as I approached the sixth decade of living. But *que sera, sera*, as the song goes. What will be, will be. None of us can predict how we will live our final days.

I hope I can grow old like Fr. Brendan. During my periodic visits to Vancouver, I would try to visit him. I would often drop by unannounced, only to be welcomed warmly and fully. He was much slower this time around. He couldn't eat by himself. His mind seemed to slip now and then. But one thing was evident. He still had that ever so attractive smile and warmth. Some may call it charm. I call it plain goodness.

At one point, he made me smile. "I miss my Guinness," he whispered. I'm sure he did. I, too, missed the chance to again invite him to the pub for a draught and a feed. Those were simple pleasures, like all pleasure should be – easy, simple, mutual.

A few weeks after that visit, friends informed me that Fr. Brendan had died. Not a surprise. I knew when I left him that day that I would probably never see him again. Commitments would prevent me from attending his funeral. My only regret.

And so, I continue confident and joy-filled at having known Fr. Brendan. He must have been in his late 70s when we first met. Thankfully, friendships have no age limit or expiry dates. They're simply gifts – gifts to be treasured and nurtured. God rest him. Fr. Brendan, pray for us.

OCTOBER

Giving Thanks for Oneself

When I lived in Vancouver, I used to see my spiritual director every three to four weeks. He lived up the Fraser River valley, in Abbotsford. I enjoyed getting out into the valley for a short visit. The three-hour return trip was well worth it – at least for my soul.

My director would usually leave me with a theme or scriptural passage to guide my prayer in the ensuing weeks. One time he suggested that I focus on the theme of thanksgiving in the context of Luke's story of the 10 lepers. Ten lepers are healed by Jesus, but only one, a Samaritan, we are told, returns to Jesus to give thanks (Luke 17:11-19).

During our next meeting, I realized something significant. I had known it for some time, I think, but to admit it to someone else took some effort.

I had to admit that I am truly thankful for who I am. An obvious sentiment, you may think. Aren't we all called to love ourselves? But think again. How do you feel about yourself? We are often plagued by so many internal voices and head talk that does less than build us up. Often, it's just the opposite. We so easily compare ourselves to one another, falling into the equally sticky pits of pride or self-deprecation. We lament the past or worry about the future.

I don't always feel on top of the world about myself. Each day has its own rhythm of ups and downs, ins and outs. But during the conversation with my spiritual director, I knew that deep within, I liked who I was – or better still, who I had become.

Now, don't get me wrong. It doesn't mean that I have it all together. Far from it. I still bite my nails. A good friend, God rest her soul, once said that I did not have the hands of a priest. "What is that supposed to mean?" I retorted. "What do the hands of a priest look like?" Maybe it was the cuts and bruises that I had sustained during my field research – as well as the poor nails, more or less attacked, that invited my friend's observation.

My feet are size seven and a half double E. That caused another friend to once query with a twinkle in his eye, "How do you manage to stand up on those tiny feet?" That I can do quite well, thank you, but I must admit that finding footwear that fits is always a challenge. One of my legs is a bit longer than the other, my spine has a slight basal curve, and I have been blessed with an extra bone in my left foot. I am not immune from sometimes hurting others – inadvertently, I hope. I can be afflicted by the same normal dose of fear, doubt and restlessness known to most people.

But, in and through it all, I like the way I've turned out. I enjoy being with myself. This has been through very little effort on my part, I will admit. Everyone has been gift – parents, teachers, friends and others. Genetics have no doubt played a role as well. Probably most important of all has been the amazing grace of God that has never abandoned me to my own destruction.

I could not have written this 10, 20 or 40 years ago. Maybe I could not have written it even a year ago. It takes time to fall in love, particularly with oneself. As we admit in the Eucharist, it is right to give God thanks and praise – thanks and praise for everything – and that means everything, even ourselves.

Fiction and Non-fiction

It's funny how we have come to classify the product of our writing. We have two broad categories: fiction and non-fiction.

Non-fiction writing includes such expressions as science, theology, biography, history, essays and the like. Fiction, on the other hand, encompasses novels, plays, short stories and other such creations of the human imagination. Non-fiction purports to deal with truth, the product of human reason and rationale. Fiction, therefore, is left with what is not true, but rather is a product, or figment, of someone's vivid imagination, a story, a parable, or the like.

Such a dualism, I think, is fatally wrong.

I know of many works of non-fiction that turned out to be false or wrong; in a word, fictitious. The author may have written with the truth in mind, but later data, experience or reflection deemed the original work to be limited, flawed or even outright wrong. The work of non-fiction turned out to be fictitious – and most such works are never heard of again.

But take a work of so-called fiction. Many of these works have become what we call classics. Think of the Greek myths, the works of William Shakespeare, the poems of T.S. Eliot, or the novels of Charles Dickens, Jane Austen or Fyodor Dostoevsky. Why do these writings, and many others, continue to persist through the ages? Why are students still required to read such works? Why are they reprinted decade after decade for new generations to enjoy? Why all this when they are simply "fiction"?

You may see where I am going. The "fiction/non-fiction" couplet is simply meaningless.

Fr. Ron Rolheiser, O.M.I., the well-known syndicated columnist, is fond of saying that the best way to learn good theology is to read good literature. I couldn't agree more. During my doctoral studies at the University of British Columbia, I found myself immersed in the novels of the so-called Catholic writer Graham Greene. I couldn't get enough of Greene as I scoured many a second-hand bookstore in search of his novels.

Graham Greene's works are deemed to be fiction, but I came to learn more about the truth of God's grace, redemption and the meaning of Christian sanctity than I may have learned from my formal courses in theology. The same could be said for the works of the American novelist Flannery O'Connor or the contemporary New Brunswick novelist David Adams Richards. And never have I read a description of the human soul better than the one found in Margaret Atwood's novel *Oryx and Crake*.

In other words, good literature deals with the stuff of life: real stuff, true stuff. It grapples with the constant questions posed by humans since the dawn of time. It deals with the truth of life. That is why we still read Homer's *Iliad* or Tolstoy's *War and Peace*.

The same problem with the notions of fiction and non-fiction apply particularly well to Sacred Scripture. With today's empirical mind, we tend to ask of Scripture, "Is it true?" or "Did it happen that way?" Such questions are generally wrong-headed. Rather than ask if Adam and Eve actually existed, we are invited to ponder the *meaning* of Adam and Eve.

The literal meaning of Scripture is important. But just as important, and maybe even more important, is the spiritual meaning of Scripture. The failure to distinguish between the form and the content of Scripture is one of the reasons for the current culture war between evolution and a literalist reading of Genesis. Such a mammoth waste of time and effort.

A Jesuit brother of mine has read Jane Austen's *Pride and Prejudice* at least 20 times. He could be called a fool if we thought of such a literary classic as "untrue." But my friend knows that Austen is writing about human truth in ways that non-fiction writing could never muster. Sometimes truth is so profound that only the imagination or the heart can fathom it – or express it.

Letters Mingle Souls

"More than kisses, letters mingle souls. For thus friends absent speak," wrote John Donne (1572–1631) in the poem "To Sir Henry Wotton."

While I would never disparage the power of the kiss, I get what John Donne says. Letters do indeed mingle souls.

At my parents' home in Newfoundland, you will find boxes chock full of letters written to me over many a year. Actual letters on paper with envelopes stamped, addressed and mailed. An increasingly rare sight in the digital age. My task – to ferret through the hundreds of letters, to keep what I wish, and to weed out what I can.

This task proved easier said than done. It only took a few letters for me to realize what a monumental task I had given myself. It would prove to be impossible.

Which letters should I keep? Which letters will I let go? Which letters need I let go?

Some letters were easy. Such were the functional notes of acquaintances or associates that held little sway – notes for which a quick email would suffice today. But then there were those other letters that held me and wouldn't let me go. Like a letter from a friend of long ago, from a time when the world and I were different. But there she was, as if it was yesterday. Across the miles and the years sprang forth memories long forgotten, dreams spoken of, hopes shared.

What rich fare lay in those cardboard boxes. The panorama of the many and varied people who defined me. Many have come and gone. Into our lives people enter, only to depart in ways that are easy and light or painful and heavy.

In some instances, contact persisted for a while, but time and distance being what they are, the letters eventually stopped. What remains are the souls living in ink on paper.

For a few, often only a select few, the letters continued. A friendship blossoms that can never know death. Such a strange, beautiful affair when two people continue to mingle their souls through the years, no matter what. Such friendships, while they can and must be nurtured, live, I think, as a spark of the Divine.

As you can see, the sifting of letters is not a job to be done quickly or lightly. At least not for me. One either takes the whole affair, encases it in cement and throws it into the depths of the sea or, as in my case, reopens, rereads and relives each letter.

Letters speak of the tapestry of one's life. The greatest of all heresies or falsehoods is the assumption that we are self-made. My letters spoke differently. The letters reminded me of the tapestry of my life stitched and woven by countless threads of intersection.

People weave themselves throughout our lives in hidden and often obscure ways. Our lives are pure gift, never predetermined, never set in stone, but living and breathing, infused by the breath of others. Our lives are crafted, built up by the many hands and voices and hearts and souls that dare enter and walk with us. We are the same for others.

Lives mingle for a short while or a lifetime. The alchemy of life makes its mark – whether tested in fire or caressed by the finest of whispers. Either way, we emerge never the same, the new alloys of life transforming us.

Despite the utility and practicality of email and the many means of social networking, I am still drawn to the pleasure of pen and paper. It's all too good to give up.

You may or may not agree with John Donne that letters mingle souls better than kisses. Both communicate the beauty of life. But in letters do absent friends indeed speak – those living and those who live on in our hearts.

Man About Town

They say you can never go back. That's invariably true, I suppose, even if I could, at times, desire otherwise.

I'm with my parents in my hometown for a visit before heading on to Kenya and Europe. I am often a bit discombobulated when I return to my native home. It takes a day or two of transition to find my new legs.

A good walk about town often helps the transition. Today, under brilliant sun and a cool, fresh breeze off the North Atlantic, I walked to the top of Signal Hill and back to my parents' home – a jaunt that took several hours.

I delight in hiking the cliffs overlooking the deep blue ocean ringed with a glaze of surging white foam on the stubborn headlands. Beyond the horizon lay the shores of Europe. An overnight flight from St. John's will take me there in only five hours.

On my walk, I passed through many memories. Institutions of the past transformed, rethought, renamed, restructured – or simply forgotten. I walked back on the Trans-Canada trail bordering the lovely Waterford River. As a boy, I dreamt of one day riding the train across the island along this same right-of-way. The affectionately and aptly named "Newfie Bullet" was finally laid to rest as the trans-province railway was removed years ago, a victim of the new Trans-Canada Highway.

The waterfront no longer welcomes the fishing boats of Spain, Portugal, Russia or Japan. I remember well the strange-smelling cigarettes of these foreign fishers, the multitude of accents and the Portuguese men playing a game of soccer on the wharf. The soccer ball would invariably end up in the drink, only to be quickly and deftly retrieved by a net at the end of a long wooden pole. The Portuguese White Fleet came prepared.

The rusty fishing boats of the past are now replaced by the tough, sturdy ships that service the booming offshore oil industry. The cod currency of the past has given way to the black gold of today.

St. John's shows off this new money in varied ways. Downtown is being transformed into fine dining establishments, high-tech offices, convention centres and expensive condos amid ongoing debates on how the city wishes to grow into the future.

I find much of the new development rather tasteless and inappropriate. The misnamed "Smart Centres" stuffed with big-box stores proliferate at the edges of town, while subdivisions spring up like unwelcome weeds, ill-planned with few or no options for local shopping, parks or an understanding of how people actually live. New roads slice the town, scarring once bucolic hillsides. Nothing seems to grow organically anymore. Quick and abundant money mesmerizes us and leads us by the nose.

I'm at home in the old part of town, the part that took years to craft, for trees to grow, for communities to form. The newfangled parts of town seem tawdry and cheap, bereft of soul and charm.

It's true that one can never go back to the same thing. I can never hope for the city of my childhood. At the same time, the old city harbours values that we forget at our peril. Maybe that's what I miss as I walk about town.

Mice and the Fountain of Youth

As I move into the second half of life, I may be forgiven for slipping into thoughts of mortality or immortality. Despite my love of the Grouse Grind trail or the British Columbia Mountaineering Club trail up North Vancouver's Grouse Mountain, it is obvious that certain parts of me don't seem to function with the same gusto as before. So, it was with a certain interest that I read a 2010 story from the Harvard Medical School where a team of researchers had managed to rejuvenate aging mice. Apparently, mice on the verge of kicking the bucket were given a new lease on life. Premature aging was reversed.

The genetically modified mice were grown without the enzyme telomerase, a situation that caused rapid premature aging. Midway through the normal lifespan of the mice, their organs had shrunk, their brains had deteriorated and the mice had lost the ability to detect noxious odours. Sound familiar? But when the researchers used a drug that reinitiated the production of telomerase, the mice bounced back to life with renewed vigour. The results of the aging process had actually reversed.

There is no doubt that telomerase is a significant factor in the aging process. Other scientists caution, however, that there is more to aging than telomerase. Furthermore, it was pointed out that this study did not consider normal aging, but aging in mice that were genetically manipulated to grow abnormally. For humans, things may be a tad more complicated.

Regardless of the legitimate arguments and cautions of the detractors, this study has gained wide attention since its recent publication. Who among us would not relish the return of some of that youthful zest and vigour?

At the same time, I cannot imagine being young forever. That could be the greatest hell on earth. At what age would I like

things to stop: 18, 25 or even 30 years? What about the prover-
bial 50-year mark? I might enjoy some of the bodily rewards of
those early years, but I'm not keen on returning to some of my
adolescent or infantile behaviours – not that we ever fully escape
them, but you know what I mean. I've covered too much ground
and suffered too much to go back in time.

Obviously, these researchers are not talking of reversing our
age or going back in time. The exciting results will no doubt spur
future research as we understand better what keeps us healthy
and wise. Life expectancies have increased from 25 to 30 years
during our cave days to a global average of 71 years (81 years in
Canada, according to 2012 data). That's quite a shift.

So let's keep on living. Each day will bear its own wisdom
in sickness and in health, in good times and in bad. Each day is
a gift. Let us live it knowing that God calls us all, including time
itself, into the eternal Love of God.

NOVEMBER

Life at the Edge

Across the leaden North Atlantic, its distinctive colour graced the waves, competing with the whitecaps. Two days in a row, the same scene. She cruised below the headlands, her white head and tail feathers bold against the grinding seas. I had seen bald eagles around Newfoundland before, but only from time to time. This was the first time I witnessed them below Signal Hill in St. John's.

Apparently, eastern Newfoundland is home to a healthy breeding population of bald eagles. The rugged headlands provide excellent nesting and perching habitat, and surrounding marine waters are rich in food.

Life happens where the land meets the oceans. For centuries, humans have been settling on the coasts. It's where the action is. Food, transport, vistas and yes, even waste management, have all been much easier on the coastal periphery.

Come to Newfoundland waters in early summer and witness the coastlands abundant with life. Humpback whales cruising north to breed and give birth. Millions of seabirds laying eggs on craggy ledges. Colourful puffins burrowing into their island-bound turf nests, after months bobbing and fishing on the deep offshore waters. With the retreat of the coastal ice, the inshore fishery begins in earnest. To mark the beginning of summer, foggy and cool weather witnesses to the orgies of capelin sperm and egg on the beach rock shores.

I don't know if that is why I gravitate to the edges – to the faraway places, to the road less travelled, to the north (or the south, if need be). Maybe it's just a matter of where I was born and baptized. I feel most at home with the land to my back and my face to the briny winds. You see far. Nothing is bounded. Hope seems assured. The seas are restless. The warmth of the land dances with the cool of the currents. Life flourishes.

Maybe it's a visceral acknowledgement that we are "not meant to be inundated by cement, asphalt, glass and metal, and deprived of physical contact with nature," as Pope Francis wrote in his encyclical on the environment, *Laudato Si'* (no. 44).

Sometimes, if we're lucky, life forces us to the edge of things. Falling in love, suffering deeply, losing our health, our mind or our memory. Failure, misunderstanding, loss.

Suddenly, we find ourselves with no way forward. We toddle on the edge, not able or wanting to go back, and seeming unable to plunge ahead. And so, on the edge, we gaze into an uncertain horizon.

Eventually, life permits us to find a way ahead. We realize that we return different from before. Hopefully, we return strengthened and encouraged.

I hope I'm not simply running away from something, from the madding crowd. But I need to fall towards the edge. I need to stand out, to stand forth into the distance. The horizon soothes and opens possibilities.

She passed below me, into the breeze mounting the coastal cliffs. I steadied myself and watched her till she passed from view.

My gaze returned to the horizon marking the pewter skies. Such moments are good for the eyes and good for the soul. Turning, I left the edge, content with its gift for today. God willing, there would be another day at the edge.

Cherish the Moment

You never know what the day will bring.

On that day, I never saw it coming. The brand-new BMW flashed before me. Metal met and buckled as we embraced in mid-street. Another statistic. Luckily, I and my passenger walked away from the wreck. I limped the car off to a safe haven and surveyed the damage. It would be judged a write-off.

The driver of the other car did not move or exit his vehicle. He was conscious, but in shock. He slowly emerged as colleagues scurried from his workplace – ironically, a collision shop.

Fault would be fully assigned to the other driver who, for some reason, miscalculated. Our thoughts often lapse. Mostly, such lapses mean little or nothing. Not this time. Who would have thought that two strangers would meet that day in a tangled twist of glass and metal in the pouring rain?

Each day of our lives is pure gift. It takes something like a car accident to bring such truths to bear.

I like to think that I consider each day as gift. My health has been strong and robust over the years. I have feared little of the misfirings and vagaries of health.

However, I have had my close calls – like the time when I decided, as a young boy, to guzzle down some anti-freeze. An attractive green, it looked just like refreshing Kool-Aid. My stomach still turns when I think of that fateful day. Rapid pumping of my stomach at the local hospital saved my bacon.

Or the time during my field research when my all-terrain vehicle decided to buck me off onto the rocky trail. All alone, miles from the cabin, as my right knee ballooned ever so nicely. I managed to limp back onto the quad and made it to my cabin just before nightfall. At the end of that summer, I was no worse for wear except for a scratched cornea, clawed by a spruce branch, and several near misses as the trees I cut decided to fall other than where I thought they would. Oh yes, I shouldn't forget the time when I was charged by a full-grown bull moose as the cow and calf looked on. Luckily, the raging bull changed his mind at the last second. I wouldn't have had a chance.

I never think much of my mortality. I still have much to do and places to see …

But brushes with death do cause one to ponder. Each day is indeed a gift. Don't take it for granted. Marvel at the spring flowers. Tell someone you love them. Visit a friend.

We never know how we will live our final moments. In the meantime, cherish each and every moment. It could be your last.

Truly God *and* Truly Human

Have you ever imagined Jesus Christ with a bad cold, warts or a backache? It's easy to think of him as above these pesky human conditions. He was God, after all.

But remember what the Council of Chalcedon (451 AD) professed centuries ago – that is, our belief in Jesus Christ as true God *and* true man.

The formulators of the classic Chalcedon creed wrote with a modest and sober clarity. For the most part, we get the fact that Jesus was truly divine. As for his humanity, however, we are often less sure of things.

In fact, Fr. Karl Rahner, S.J., a celebrated 20th-century Jesuit theologian, admitted that most Christians were probably "crypto-Monophysites." By this he meant that when it came down to it, most of us lived a faith that emphasized the divine nature of Christ to the detriment of Christ's human nature. On the other hand, some Christians have taken just the opposite perspective, emphasizing the humanity of Christ to the detriment of his divinity.

If Jesus Christ were truly human, and this we profess, then all the human bodily experiences he had, being as they are of God, are fundamentally good and as human and as common as yawning and burping.

The beauty of Christian theology is its universal or catholic character. It's never "either/or," but rather "both/and."

The "both/and" approach is also helpful when we talk of the resurrection of Jesus Christ.

Scripture is a constant witness to the resurrection of the full person of Jesus Christ – body and soul, if you will. What the resurrected state means, I am not able to say. Nor can anyone else, for that matter.

But one thing is obvious. The resurrected Christ is the wounded Christ. To his astonished disciples, Jesus says, "Touch me and see; for a ghost does not have flesh and bones as you see that I have" (Luke 24:39). The resurrected Christ walked with his disciples, appeared to them, ate breakfast with them.

All this to say, I think, that in and through the resurrection of Jesus Christ, the human body, indeed all matter and all creation, is transformed in the loving, eternal embrace of God, the Giver of Life. And that includes everything – warts and all.

The Blank Page

I've heard of writer's block, but thought myself immune from such a malady.

For most of the time, writing this book came rather easily. I had an idea, an idea that animated me, an idea for which I could find words. One day all that changed.

For some reason, my mind became a *tabula rasa*, a blank slate that seemed to bear no words whatsoever. Pressure built as I approached the deadline for submission. In the meantime, other demands called for my attention. What to do?

I was at a loss for words, with no time to think straight, and new demands continuing to crop up all the time. So, I thought, why not simply write on being lost?

I don't know about you, but I'm not very good at multitasking. My mind likes rather simple, focused tasks. I like going into depth with a task or project. I love research that takes me into the minutiae, into a depth that is not obvious at first glance. I am drawn deep into the wonder of the world. Maybe that is why I have always felt called to a life of scientific research.

There is a temptation these days, with the internet and social media, to rest on the surface of life, to accept superficiality at the expense of depth.

Think of the prodigious amounts of information at our fingertips via Google. Never did we have such ability to express and publish our thoughts and ideas. Blogs, tweets and websites abound. Social revolutions are fuelled by the cellphone, and gone are the days when most of us can get by without a smart phone.

Don't get me wrong. I love my iPhone, and frankly would not know what to do without it. My lichen research would be seriously or even fatally hampered without rapid internet access and dependable online access to the electronic scientific journals at the University of Toronto library.

But I cannot get myself to tweet my life away. I am happy to have no friends – on Facebook, that is. I enjoy the feel (and smell) of a good book. I take pen and paper to hand when I wish to write to a good friend. I relish the rigour of wading through reasoned, critical thinking. I cannot, and simply don't wish to, handle the deluge of information that swirls throughout cyberspace.

All this is too dizzying for me. Friendship is a gift, often hard earned, and challenging in what can be painful ways. And good friendships can often be counted on one hand, never counted in the thousands. Information is one thing, but wisdom and dialogue and reasoned thought are another.

I long for depth in thought and imagination. Maybe that is why many aspects of social media rub me the wrong way. As I said above, I don't enjoy having too much vying for my attention. My mind is too simple for that. I get great joy from focus and depth. I eschew the myriad voices clamouring for my attention.

So, here I am. The blank slate has taken shape and form. Thank you for following my train of thought yet one more time. My mind may be blank at times, but that doesn't prevent me from at least trying to sow a few thoughtful words to paper.

Viagra and the Spiritual Life

They tell me it can do wonders. I have no reason to doubt it.

For the more scientifically minded, it is known as sildenafil citrate. Most of us know it as Viagra. It acts by inhibiting the enzyme cyclic guanosine monophosphate (cGMP)-specific phosphodiesterase type 5, which delays degradation of cGMP. Apparently, Viagra was originally developed to treat hypertension and angina, but was eventually marketed as a successful treatment for erectile dysfunction. Viagra increases blood flow to the penis, allowing a good erection to be maintained for up to four hours.

Four hours – that seems like a long time. But what do I know about such things?

Often, we may sense that we need a bit of spiritual Viagra. We may feel that our spiritual lives need a bit of a kick-start or boost. We sense that we have grown distant from God. We seem lackadaisical in our prayer or in our spiritual devotions. The God of former times seems nowhere to be found. We may feel adrift, like dust in the wind.

Fr. Ron Rolheiser, O.M.I., the celebrated spiritual writer, likes to say that "lost is a place, too." I firmly believe that.

When I think of the times in my life when I seemed somewhat adrift, without a compass, maybe even terribly lost, I can now see the hand of God in the midst of it all.

Scripture gives us that wonderful icon of being lost – the desert. It was only in the dry, weary desert that the people of Israel came to yearn for the living water of God. I love how the psalmist so eloquently expresses that yearning: "My flesh faints for you as in a dry and weary land where there is no water" (Psalm 63:1). We often need to be swallowed by a whale, carried through the depths of the deep and spewed forth in places we least hoped for or expected. Unless you get lost, you'll never come to realize how much you long to be found.

When you experience spiritual dysfunction, don't run too quickly towards the many forms of spiritual Viagra. They may satisfy in the short term as you bounce through life full of vim and vigour. But you won't be able to sustain it. The spiritual life looks to the long haul, not a quick fix.

And because the spiritual life looks to the long haul, because it knows that there is a time for everything, be gentle with those times of doubt or darkness that may befall you. You may feel lost, but God knows exactly where you are. Never doubt that. Keep praying, keep awake, keep vigilant, for you never know the hour or the day when you will once again break into the divine goodness and freshness of life.

DECEMBER

The Cosmic Christ

Jesus Christ is more than Jesus of Nazareth. The mystery of Jesus Christ has what may be called a cosmic dimension. Resting solidly on the witness of the New Testament, particularly the often-cited Colossians hymn (Colossians 1:15-20) and Ephesians 1:9-10, the notion of the cosmic Christ flows from the heart of the Church's liturgy and is a necessary consequence of our belief in Jesus Christ as Lord and Saviour of all. Scripture witnesses to Jesus Christ "in" and "through" whom all things were created (1 Corinthians 8:6, Colossians 1:16, Hebrews 1:2, John 1:3) and in whom all things will be transformed (Colossians 1:20, Ephesians 1:10, Hebrews 1:3). In Christ, all things hold together (Colossians 1:17).

In other words, Christ is intimately related to the entire cosmos, and the entire cosmos finds its meaning in Christ. Christ is the alpha and the omega, the beginning and the end. Christ is the beginning of creation as the Word of God and the completion of creation as the incarnation of the Word. The cosmos, the universe, all that ever was and ever will be, is governed by a "Christic" structure.

We need to liberate Christ from the man Jesus so that Christ may truly be the heart of creation, the inner structure of the universe, the centring principle of evolution, the fulfillment of an evolutionary universe.

In St. John Paul II's final encyclical on the Eucharist, his 2003 *Ecclesia de Eucharistia*, the Pope noted that "the Eucharist is always in some way celebrated *on the altar of the world*. It unites heaven and earth. It embraces and permeates all creation. The Son of God became man in order to restore all creation, in one supreme act of praise, to the One who made it from nothing" (no. 8). This can only be if Christ is truly cosmic in character. Only then will Jesus Christ be truly worthy of our praise as the Saviour of the world.

Why Did God Become Incarnate?

Christmas is a celebration of the mystery of the incarnation of God in the flesh and blood of Jesus Christ. In the mass on Christmas Day, we remember these words from John's Gospel: "And the Word became flesh and lived among us ..." (John 1:14).

In the incarnation, we are faced with an incomprehensible mystery: that the Creator God of the billons of stars in the universe, the Unnamed One, the One whom humans could never see face to face, becomes visible in the flesh and blood of Jesus Christ.

Through this so-called hypostatic union, Jesus Christ becomes the "image of God" (2 Corinthians 4:4). And this image is firmly grounded in materiality. The flesh of Jesus is the flesh of the dynamic, evolving universe. As fully human, Jesus came from the humus of the earth and the stuff of the cosmos. As fully divine, Jesus proclaims that the material world is central in the order of salvation. By fully embracing the humanity of Jesus, the Word definitively accepts the salvation of creation, grounds God's relationship in the world and proclaims all creation to be good.

The incarnation is a cosmic event – the central event of not only human history, but of cosmic history as well. In and through the incarnation, the entire creation is transfigured in the sense that it becomes more than it is. As part of the cosmos, the finite body of Jesus Christ is transfigured to become the fullness of the presence of God. In the incarnation, we witness the destiny of the entire cosmos. The world, in effect, becomes transfigured and divinized by virtue of the incarnation, which according to Jesuit theologian Fr. Karl Rahner, S.J., in his 1966 book *Theological Investigations*, "appears as the necessary and permanent beginning of the divinization of the world as a whole" (p. 161).

But why did the incarnation come about? One strand of Christian thought that has dominated our discourse is that Christ's incarnation is a remedy for our sin.

Another tradition, however, suggests that God would have become incarnate even in the absence of human sin. It was God's intention from the beginning to give God's self to creation in the incarnation. In other words, the incarnation is central to the purpose of God's creation. By this way of thinking, the life, suffering, death and resurrection of Jesus Christ are not add-ons to creation, but are at the very heart and purpose of creation. The incarnation is not primarily a corrective to a creation that went wrong, but the first manifestation of the purpose of all creation. This way of thinking, rooted in Franciscan theology, is well articulated in the writings of the contemporary Franciscan friar Fr. Richard Rohr, O.F.M.

While not denying the value of the traditional focus on incarnation as remedy for sin, deeper reflection on the self-bestowal of God in and through creation merits our attention. In reflecting on this, we make the wondrous and amazing claim that God's gift of himself in creation is the very core of the world's reality.

Christmas at the Monastery

The major religious orders have had their filial tensions throughout the centuries. It got bad in the 16th century, as Jesuit and Dominican theologians squabbled over the relationship between God's grace and our free will. Eventually, the debates were ordered stopped by several popes. An agreement ensued where, upon the death of the general superior of either order, the living general of the other order would preside at the funeral mass. That's one way to get siblings back on speaking terms.

Such squabbles were completely forgotten one Christmas when a group of three Jesuits left the comforts of Point Grey, Vancouver, to venture north into the valley of the Squamish River. Their mission? To seek out Queen of Peace Monastery, a new Dominican foundation in the north end of the archdiocese of Vancouver.

Composed of Dominican nuns from around the world, the contemplative community is the product of a call from the former Dominican Master, Fr. Timothy Radcliffe, O.P., for a Dominican monastery in British Columbia. After some time in Surrey and Langley, B.C., the sisters finally settled on a lovely spot in the Squamish valley.

At first, they lived in temporary quarters; their new monastery was completed in 2012. The south-facing windows of the chapel face onto the majestic Tantalus Mountains, complete with expansive glaciers towering above temperate rainforests of yellow cedar, subalpine fir and mountain hemlock.

Monastics generally have a profound sense of place and time. The nuns are no exception. They are in it for the long haul. They wish to stay in the valley for a long time. The monastery was constructed with that deep sense of place, time and beauty. The forested Squamish valley, sheltering mountains and glaciers, lichen and moss-covered granite outcrops, mountain streams – all these define the feel and setting of the sisters' monastic home.

We were warmly and generously welcomed. Gatherings around a glowing fireplace with delicious home-cooked meals, homemade apple pie with the contours of Mount Baker, women of intellect, humour and interest, the warmth of the nicely apportioned chapel, a simplicity infused with joy.

We managed some manly activity by splitting mounds of dried spruce and fir for the sisters' fireplace and woodstoves. An evening stroll under the brilliant Milky Way in the dark skies brought us to our senses.

Those Dominican and Jesuit debates on the meaning of God's grace and our free will have long since disappeared and are, for the most part, forgotten. Over Christmas, for a few days at least, some Dominican women and a few Jesuit men managed to spend some time together in relative peace.

O Christmas Tree, O Christmas Tree

The centuries-old tradition of the Christmas tree holds special meaning for human culture. The winter solstice (around December 21) marks the period of the shortest day in the northern hemisphere. It was at this dark time of year that northern European Christians, particularly in Germany, focused on the symbolism of life as they set up evergreen Christmas trees in their homes. The evergreen branches of the conifer in the warmth of the home acted as a needed antidote to the cold and death of winter.

In 1982, St. John Paul II instituted the raising of a Christmas tree in St. Peter's Square at the Vatican. The first Vatican Christmas Tree was a silver fir (*Abies alba*) from the Alban Hills, east of Rome. The 2016 tree was a 25-metre Norway spruce (*Picea abies*) from Trentino, a mountainous region in northeast Italy. Each year, cities from all over Europe vie for the privilege of gifting Vatican City with a Christmas tree.

One year, the Christmas tree in our chapel at the University of British Columbia was a young Douglas fir (*Pseudotsuga menziesii*) from the forests above West Vancouver. This species is misnamed, with true firs belonging to the genus *Abies*. Douglas fir is named after David Douglas (1799–1834), a Scottish botanist who carried out a botanical exploration of the Pacific Northwest in 1824. The traditional Christmas tree of eastern Canada is the lovely and fragrant balsam fir (*Abies balsamea*). It was first described by the famous Swedish botanist Carl Linnaeus in 1753.

Whatever conifer species you may have as a Christmas tree, rejoice in the new life of Jesus Christ about to erupt into our world.

Marked by Our Surroundings

Picture yourself standing up on the Canadian Prairies or the Great Plains of the United States. Would that help you to perceive of the Earth as round? Probably not. As far from mountains as one can get on the North American continent, the flat interior lands stretch the imagination far and distant. Big sky country. Prone to so many long droughts that trees, and even shrubs, have a difficult time taking root. The prairie grasses run the length and breadth of the land.

I have never lived on the Prairie, only passed through for a day or more. Even the notion of passing through may be an exaggeration. More like dropping down into the Prairie, and then only in the dead of winter. I run a hazard, therefore, in attempting to even think of the meaning of the Prairie, let alone write about it. That should be left to writers rooted in the grasslands, like Sharon Butala and Trevor Herriot.

That being said, maybe growing up on the edge of the North Atlantic has earned me some Prairie stripes. In both places, it's hard to stand up to see the roundness of the world. Horizoned sky that's bigger than life. Sky that arches its back to flatten the world.

Why couldn't the Earth be flat? Why can't the sun rise over the eastern edge to fall away on the western edge, marking the end of day? How could I ever stand tall enough to peer over the edge to view the everlasting curve of things?

I suppose the same question could be asked of every land and sea. I'm sure that if I lived long and travelled well the Great Plains, I would come to perceive more than flatness. I would come to witness the Prairie's curve, life and dip. The way even the slightest topographical bend or lift ripples farther than the eye could see. Tilt the prairie ground a little and the water will flow.

Given enough time, I would come to witness the myriad meanings of Prairie. The words that only a prairie can speak. The sounds that only a prairie wind can blow. The stillness that only a prairie can offer.

I suppose that every place on earth has something to offer. I wonder if that is what Pope Benedict XVI meant when he wrote in his 2009 encyclical *Caritas in Veritate* that "nature expresses a design of love and truth" and that "it too is a 'vocation'" (no. 48). A vocation to utter, to vocalize, its uniqueness and gift. Or as Judeo-Christians have come to acknowledge, that all of creation is a Word of God. Divinity materialized. Divinity incarnate.

Imagine human culture having originated and developed on the moon. What kind of music would we have created? What literature and poetry would we have written? No doubt our lunar landscape would have shaped our minds in its own lunar way.

But one thing is sure. Our lunar homeland would have shaped the human mind and creativity differently from that of Earth.

I grew up not among the grasses of the dry prairie but among the wet, humid green mosses of the coastal boreal forests of Newfoundland. Flush and vibrant green, turgid with rain and fog, the boreal mosses offered not an inch of space to other would-be companions. Spruce and fir standing in unbroken carpets of bryophytes with names like *Hylocomium splendens, Pleurozium schreberi, Sphagnum girgensohnii*. Spilling over, one on top of the other, to create spongy beds, cushions of life and nutrients for all. Growing ever so slowly in yearly increments, edging forward vertically, diagonally and horizontally. A relentless creep of moss.

To the boreal moss and the Prairie grass, the Earth is indeed flat. Life is bounded to a horizon marked in metres, or even centimetres. As humans, we're probably no different. We're marked by our surroundings. Immediate surroundings like prairie, forest and sea. Our culture is defined greatly by our "nature," by our environment, by that which surrounds us.

I feel blessed to be marked by the barrens, the mossy forests and the fog-strewn, rocky coasts of the North Atlantic. I know that I continue to be marked by so many other places that I have come to call home. We are never immune to such markings. They mark us for life, even when we are unaware.